THE
Fruit
IS NOT FOR
THE
TREE

HOW TO BE FORGIVING, FREE AND FRUITFUL WHEN OFFENSES COME

THE *Fruit* IS NOT FOR THE TREE

HOW TO BE FORGIVING, FREE AND FRUITFUL WHEN OFFENSES COME

C. D. DUDLEY

MEWE

Love is the more excellent way

Lithonia, GA

Publisher:
MEWE, LLC
Lithonia, GA
www.mewellc.com

The Fruit Is Not for the Tree
First Edition

ISBN: 9780998828190

Library of Congress Control Number: 2017913501

Printed in the United States of America.

To my Lord and Savior Jesus Christ for being the ultimate example of humility, love and forgiveness.

To my mother who had the strength to endure so much in your lifetime. Your latter days will be your best days.

To my children who have loved and supported me; I love you more than you will ever know.

Table of Contents

Introduction

Making our way through life comes with a myriad of events, emotions and consequences. As we navigate, we encounter people and situations that make us happy, sad, furious and touchy. And, truthfully, some people seem to be experts at being offensive with their words and actions. We come across people like that every day – in our homes, workplaces, social settings and even at church.

Naturally, we desire the good opinions of others and like to hear positive things about ourselves and what we do. Moreover, we want what we believe we deserve. But when those things are not forthcoming – the problems begin. None of us likes to be disrespected, unappreciated, betrayed, deceived, treated unfairly, ignored or criticized. Period. And so, we take offense.

Consequently, we exhibit typical human behavior to fight for our rights, set the record straight, and go full steam in a "tit for tat" battle. Unfortunately, more often than not, we end up wasting our time and energy incessantly dwelling on the offense and the offender, which causes more scars than the offense itself.

Taking offense and thirsting for revenge affect us mentally, physically and spiritually, making it hard to let go and move forward. The anger harbored within takes root and is aggravated by the devil constantly reminding us of the offense and the offender. Day by day we are battered and consumed with thoughts of how we were wronged and offended. "Why did she say that to me?" "I was so good to her; how could she repay me like that?" "Are you going to let him get away with it?" How many times have you rehashed all the offenses that have been committed against you? How many people are you still angry with and have not forgiven?

For each, you take the bait of offense that does more harm than good. The bitterness, resentment, and unforgiveness rooted within are unhealthy and detrimental to life. Inevitably, you can only bear fruits of pain and hurt because the principles of life dictate you can only produce what has been planted. Without realizing it, you may soon become barren, unattractive, unapproachable and useless.

Know that satan sets the bait of offense to immobilize and make us ineffective in the Kingdom of God. He knows that, when we are crippled by our own emotions and allow the roots of bitterness to grow in our lives, we will not be effective witnesses. If people cannot see the love of God revealed through us, our words have no effect. It's our actions that matter. That's why Jesus implored His disciples to let their lights shine in this dark world so that men may see and glorify Him: "*Let your light so shine before men, that they may see your good works, and glorify your Father which is in heaven*" (Matthew 5:16). When we do not take offense, people will see the divine grace of God in us being manifested outwardly. Our words, actions and lifestyles will demonstrate that there is something different about us that's worth having, and they will be compelled to know more about the Kingdom of God. Christ is ready to draw them unto Himself.

Sometimes we are offended by something that was not even designed to offend us. Offenses are words or actions that are *intended* to cause anger, resentment or hatred. At the same time, sometimes the words of others are not meant as an offense; instead, they are a correction, a teaching or a word of wisdom.

We must avoid getting offended because we do not like what is being said, even though it is for our good. It is true that correction and the truth oftentimes hurt, and we may very well get angry, but we get off track with God when we take offense and react in a way that is not pleasing to God. The Bible says, *"Be ye angry, and sin not"* (Ephesians 4:26). Do not take the bait and get trapped by the enemy. I will be providing more details about offenses throughout the book.

In comparison, there are people who do intend to cause hurt, anger or resentment with their words or actions. We should still not take offense. We should RESPOND to these situations according to the Word of God as well.

The primary purpose of this book is to share how we should respond to deliberate offenses. There are times when we should forgive and be reconciled and there are also times when we should forgive and walk away – in some cases run!

You can move beyond offense to a productive life that blooms and bears good fruit. Your life can overflow with goodness, kindness, love and peace. If you want to prevent yourself from taking offense, and experience a life that compels others to you because of your beauty – you can. The fruit you bear will be your attraction; they will be the visible signs of God's divine grace working in you and expressing itself through your words and actions.

In this book, you will discover the power within to overcome and flourish. You will learn how to get rid of the insecurities that tempt you to take offense and you will begin to value God's opinion of you, above all else.

As you feed on God's Word and drink from the springs of living water, you will bear fruit bountifully and participate in abundant living that attracts others. Why wither and dry up with bitterness when you can bloom as you please God, bear fruit in every good work and increase in His knowledge?

As you turn each page, may you desire the good fruit of the Holy Spirit and disregard the offense. God has chosen and appointed you to flourish: "*Ye have not chosen me, but I have chosen you, and ordained you, that ye should go and bring forth fruit, and that your fruit should remain: that whatsoever ye shall ask of the Father in my name, he may give it you*" (John 15:16). God's power working in and through you will change your life and those around you.

When you get to a place where your focus or desire is for the persons who offended you to be closer to God and to be everything God wants them to be, then you have reached a new level of maturity in your faith. Your peace will come quicker when you are not self-centered and have a heart for others.

It takes a mature person to forgive someone who has been offensive. We have to change our focus, and desire for others to be closer to God – even those who offend us. Let's take the focus off ourselves and desire to be fruitful for the benefit of others, knowing and trusting that God will take care of us in the process!

Oh, to be like a tree…!

- C. D. Dudley

Preface

All my life, I have been fascinated by nature. Trees are especially awe-inspiring to me. The more I look at their beauty and benefits, the more I realize that God created the perfect analogy for me to help you understand why it is important for you to "keep happy" in the midst of offense. Now, it's true that maintaining happiness does not always mean forgiving someone and then expecting everything to be restored the way it was. Sometimes it just means forgiving someone and moving on – no longer holding the other person guilty or thinking that he or she owes you anything.

The Fruit Is Not for the Tree is about understanding that we are crucial to Kingdom building and that our varied experiences or the way we live our lives are part of the process. In other words, we come to a place of maturity, realizing that our lives are not just about us, but also about how effective we are at being part of Christ's process to draw others to Himself. We lift Him up in the way we live our lives so that others will see Him in us and want to also know Him.

Have you ever seen a tree eat its own fruit? No. A tree produces fruit for others to consume. How selfless! Don't get me wrong, the tree still benefits in the process of the fruit being produced. Just having good fruit on its branches is an indication that the tree is healthy. It was formed from good seeds, which were nourished during the fruit-bearing process. In the same way, we are blessed as we walk according to the Word of God to produce the fruit of the Spirit in our lives so that others will be compelled to Christ. The Bible says that the man who delights in the law of the Lord shall be like *"a tree planted by the rivers of water, that bringeth forth his fruit in his season; his leaf also shall not wither; and whatsoever he doeth shall prosper"* (Psalm 1:3). We are prosperous in the way we live and we are also prosperous in our witness because of the fruit we bear.

I know, perhaps better than a great many people, what it means to suffer from offenses. Some of my childhood memories revolve around how I never felt good enough, pretty enough or light-colored enough because that was viewed as beautiful back in the day. Growing up dark-skinned was not easy for many children back then, and having short hair made it worse – many of the insults, jokes and bullying I lived through came from the fact that I was what they called "bald-headed" for some parts of my childhood. Over the years our society has done a better job of embracing women wearing shorter and natural hair styles, but back in the day, for me, it was something that caused me such great pain that I hid within myself.

Growing up in the projects, we would sometimes get our hair done in the kitchen. I remember going from the straightening comb to a perm to a Jheri curl, and my hair ended up unhealthy and terribly broken off. I was the butt of countless jokes, which I remember to this day. Being talked about – being offended – was so painful, but I learned how to hide my feelings. Honestly, the pain of the jokes is no longer there, mainly, because I worked so hard to grow some hair so people could "coo" over the fact that this dark girl had "nice hair." It was something about hearing people, especially family and people back home, talk about how "nice" my hair was when they would see me. Sadly, I was still bound by my past and the stigma that something was wrong with short hair.

In addition to having short hair, I was also the darkest of my mother's children, which was very challenging. Normally, dark-skinned babies are born with lighter skin, then they turn the color of their ears after a short time. Well, I came out dark, with my face the same color as my ears – no transition period for me! For some reason, it was a big deal for babies to come out with lighter skin. People wanted to know about that feature the most when they inquired about someone's new baby, even though they might have been too polite to ask outright. I was called "black" so much that I grew numb from the pain that stuck to me.

It was my elementary school principal, Dr. Glass, who taught me how to feel good about myself despite my looks and economic situation. During morning announcements, she used to make us say, "I am somebody and I will always be somebody!" She helped me understand that I was somebody special and it didn't matter what other people called me or what they thought about me. I realized that black was beautiful and I was indeed a chocolate beauty. This new mindset helped, but it did not solve my problems totally.

According to other people, I had three things that were going against me instead of for me: dark-skinned, bald-headed and poor. My childhood was a battle— mainly in my mind, because I had to coach myself daily not to listen to the meanness around me. Well, that did not work as well as I wished. I became something of a "weeble wobble," in that I would sometimes cave in because of all the hurt, but I would always get back up and continue moving forward.

Yes, I began to understand that I was special. But, even though I learned to numb myself to insults and pretend that words didn't hurt me, I dealt with all the hurt in ways that were not good. Excelling and proving myself became my way out, my way of dealing with the brokenness. As I got older, I found myself in unhealthy relationships. You see, I always wanted to have a relationship because it was also a way of escape. I ostracized myself from people who could have loved me properly. I did not know how to make healthy connections, to allow myself to love and to accept love. I was deeply offended by people who helped me by treating me like I was a "project," not worthy of honor. They talked down to me in condescending and sometimes disrespectful tones. I trusted no one, feeling that no one was sincere in their attempts to be part of my life. How could they be, when I did not have the trust or desire to connect with them? I was afraid. Fear had me around the neck, choking the very life out of me, and I was too hurt and ashamed to cry out for help. I never said what I wish I could have: "Help! I'm hurting and I don't want to pretend anymore. I want to have healthy relationships. I want to move past the hurt and not harbor any ill feelings towards another."

Eventually, I made the decision to channel all the emotions I had into the energy I needed to succeed in life. Only at an older age did I realize that ignoring and misunderstanding what I truly needed had merely pacified me; but it had not addressed the problem and put it behind me. So, I remained locked in my child self for a long time. Nobody can really expect a child to know that love and forgiveness are the keys to overcoming an offense. A child hasn't even learned how to deal with the emotions and feelings that come as a result of hurt. Instead of reacting in anger or violence, a child has to be taught how to love and forgive. That's a hard-enough lesson for a child, but harder to learn later in life.

Admittedly, I almost didn't mention in my book where I grew up for part of my childhood and some of the things I'd experienced living there because it was one of the most dangerous projects in the city of Atlanta. Some even used to call it "Little Vietnam." From our porch, I saw family fights, drug deals, stabbings, and even shootings. I will never forget watching a man get shot while he was running and then die while lying in the street. For some reason, I wasn't afraid of the neighborhood, because of the families who lived around us and helped to look after us. When we went into the house, it was a refuge away from all of the things that were going on outside. I wasn't ashamed of where I lived at first as it was all I knew. However, as I got older and I began to interact with people outside of our neighborhood, they would always react with a bit of shock when I told them where I lived. So, I grew ashamed and I kept it to myself because I wanted to avoid "that look" and the comments that followed.

As I was writing this book, God said to me, "Everything that you've been through, every place of lack, every disappointment, every hurt that you have experienced, those things are working for your good. Those things are working to mold you into the person I've called you to be – a person of compassion, a person of change. When you fully accept who you are, then and only then will you be able to walk in your true calling."

So, I had to do what God told me to do; I had to add my stories, although painful, to this book. I cried through it, but I did it! Because of what I've been through, I'm getting to a place in my life where God is able to use me to reach a dying world for His Kingdom without judgment, to reach them with the spirit of love regardless of their situation, regardless of their financial status, regardless of their socio-economic status, regardless of what they look like or smell like.

I'm thankful for everything that I've been through. Every hurt, every disappointment, every offense, every shortcoming, I thank You, God, for every one of them. Those things have made me into the person I am. I am not ashamed of who I am. I am not ashamed of where I come from. I am not ashamed of what I have been through. I am not ashamed of every imperfection and every blemish that I have.

Please understand, I have "not arrived." I still make mistakes and struggle in certain areas of unforgiveness, but I declare that my latter days will be better than my former days because, although, I still mess up from time to time, I have purposed not to give up and I am determined not to take the bait when it comes to offense. The more I walk in love and forgiveness, the more beautiful I become – on the inside and outside. It amazes me how God makes me more and more attractive the older I become. I know it's because of the change that is happening on the inside.

I am living my best days!

Through studying the Word and spending time with God, I know that we are to forgive and pray for people who offend us because, more than likely, they are hurting and just refuse to be free or do not know how. Furthermore, there are others who observe how we respond to life's circumstances, and they will either be drawn to Christ as we lift Him up in our lives or they will see us acting contrary to the Word and turn away.

This journey is so much bigger than us.

- C. D. Dudley

CHAPTER 1

Understanding the Fruit

God expects His children to be fruitful, which means to be productive in multiplying or expanding. He told Adam in Genesis 1:22, *"Be fruitful, and multiply, and fill the waters in the seas, and let fowl multiply in the earth."* In the same chapter, the Bible states, *"And God blessed them, and God said unto them, Be fruitful, and multiply, and replenish the earth, and subdue it: and have dominion over the fish of the sea, and over the fowl of the air, and over every living thing that moveth upon the earth"* (Genesis 1:28). For God to state, *"be fruitful and multiply"* twice in the same chapter and then several times throughout Genesis, it must have been important for Him to ensure that the command was received.

The fruit we produce are our actions, our thoughts and also our words. The fruit can be either good or bad depending on the seed that was used to bring it forth. The Bible says, *"Even so every good tree bringeth forth good fruit; but a corrupt tree bringeth forth evil fruit"* (Matthew 7:17).

The fruit we produce is our actions, our thoughts and our words.

The Fruit of the Spirit

The good fruit we produce is called the fruit of the Spirit. More specifically, it is *"love, joy, peace, longsuffering, gentleness, goodness, faith, Meekness, temperance: against such there is no law"* (Galatians 5:22-23). The fruit of the

Spirit indicates that it is the Holy Spirit working in us to produce what God can use to show forth His presence in us.

It is important to also understand that it is the seed of the Word of God, planted on the good ground of our hearts that also helps us to produce the good fruit of love, joy, peace and so on. In other words, the Holy Spirit enables us as we walk in obedience to the Word of God to produce fruit that the Lord will use to draw others to Him and expand His Kingdom.

Since our fruit is used to expand the Kingdom of God, we are better witnesses because the Kingdom is being demonstrated in our lives. When people see us loving others, showing joy in spite of our circumstances, and walking in peace, they will want to know the reason behind our love, joy and peace.

This curiosity opens the door for us to tell them about our Lord and Savior, who has made it possible for us to walk in the fruit of the Spirit.

I am from the country and anybody who knows me well is aware that I like eating green plums. I do not mean just eating plums; I like eating green plums with salt. That's a big thing for me. When I am driving through the countryside, if I see a tree with green plums, I pull over and pick some on the side of the road.

Our lives should have the same effect on people that the green plum tree has on me. People should be attracted to and love what they see, so much so it makes them step over, stop over, pull over and do whatever it takes to get what we have.

They may have issues in their lives, too, but, because they see something appealing on our tree, they will forge their way to get it. I am so thankful that fruit can come from our lives so that people will be attracted to and desire to have the same thing.

Are You Being Picked on?

Don't be surprised to find yourself being "picked on" as you live according to the Word of God. We should have fruit in our lives that that will attract people to the Kingdom of God. When the seed of the Word is planted in the good ground of our hearts and is received, it will bring forth fruit – fruit that is compelling to others (See Mark 4:20).

Growing up, I remember for the most part that witnessing to others was telling people about their sins – drunkenness, fornication, lying and whatever they were doing wrong. It was basically warning people of the terror of hell and the prospect of spending eternity there if they did not repent. It was serious.

However, what I've learned is that we serve a loving and forgiving God. He sent His Son, Jesus, to die on the cross for us because He loved us so much, even while we were yet sinners. And so, as we witness, we have to do it in that same spirit of love. I also learned that we can witness with our lives – lives that attract others to the ways of God.

Understanding the Fruit

It is necessary to understand how important spreading the Gospel is. Without beating people over the head with the Bible, we can share the message of salvation by our very lives. When people see how we carry ourselves, our attitudes, behaviors and godly lifestyles, they will see Christ manifested in us.

Our righteous living will attract them to us, and Jesus, our Lord, will, in turn, draw them to Him. The fruit of our lives will express the God in us.

In Mark 4, we find four different types of ground and their conditions: the wayside ground, the stony ground, the thorny ground, and the good ground. Good fruit will only come forth if the seed of the Word is planted on good ground. I will talk more about the types of ground in the next chapter.

Fruit is produced as a direct result of whatever has been planted in our hearts, either good or bad. That's why it is important not to allow offenses to take control of your mind. If your mind is controlled by offenses, you will be consumed by the thought of what was done to you. Playing offensive experiences over and over again in your mind affects your heart and may cause you to react in a negative way because of your emotional baggage.

Not only does taking an offense and unforgiveness affect your heart and emotions, but they also may affect you physically. Studies show that stress and worry cause ulcers, hypertension and other physical ailments. In an article by Lorie Johnson, she states, "unforgiveness is classified in medical books as a disease. According to Dr. Steven Standiford, chief of surgery at the Cancer

Treatment Centers of America, refusing to forgive makes people sick and keeps them that way."[1]

That's why you should never allow offenses to control your mind. Guarding your heart and keeping it in a good condition is essential if you want to bring forth fruit when the Word is planted in good ground. If the ground, which represents the heart, is not good, you will not bear any fruit.

Matthew 7:16 begins by saying, *"Do people pick ...?"* I must stop right there. Those are just three words. Many times, I hear people say, "Well, I do not care what people think. I do not care about people. I do not care about their opinions." But the truth is you need to care what people see and think to a certain extent. What people think and see should concern us because we want to be – we should be – witnesses. People should be attracted to something in our lives that will bring them out of darkness.

The fruit we bear is part of our witness.

So, there is nothing wrong with people picking on us. If our fruit is appealing, people will want to pick from our tree. Picking on us is in God's plan.

> *Do people pick grapes from thornbushes, or figs from thistles? Likewise, every good tree bears good fruit, but a bad tree bears bad fruit. A good tree cannot bear bad fruit, and a bad*

tree cannot bear good fruit. Every tree that does not bear good fruit is cut down and thrown into the fire. Thus, by their fruit you will recognize them (Matthew 7:16-20).

Mark the words *"Every tree"* in *"Every tree that does not bear good fruit is cut down and thrown into the fire."*

God expects us all to bear fruit and not just any type of fruit; He expects us to bear good fruit. Remember, the only way you're going to grow good fruit on your tree is if you start with the right seed – the Word of God. That's what you ought to plant into the good ground of your heart.

Now, I am being picked on for a different reason. I have substance in my life…I have good fruit in my life…so that, if you pick it, it will cause you to love when you do not want to love, show kindness to someone you feel may not be deserving, and be gentle to someone who displays rudeness.

So, it's alright. Go on, pick on me.

God Expects Us to Be Fruitful

What did Jesus do to the fig tree when He walked past it? The fig tree is supposed to bear fruit under its leaves, but this particular tree was barren. So, Jesus cursed it. He expects us to be fruitful. He expects our hearts to be in good condition so that we can receive the Word and bear fruit.

Our God is forgiving, loving and merciful.

Don't be trapped, tricked or bamboozled. That's exactly what an offense does. It traps you, it snaps you, and it holds you in that position. Like a mouse caught in a trap, you cannot move. That's where the devil wants you to be. He wants you to be in a state of immobility, so you cannot run this race for Christ…so you cannot tell anybody about Christ because you cannot move. If the enemy is occupying your mind and thoughts, you do not have the peace you need to be fruitful and fulfill the things of God.

But, although you are made helpless in the trap of offense, unfruitful in that condition, God has a way of healing and releasing you through His Word so that you can live a life that is fruitful and effective in witnessing to others.

Our God is forgiving, loving and merciful. Since we are made in His image, we, too, should exemplify the same characteristics. When we are walking in gossip and negativity, we are not being fruitful. There is no place for gossiping and talking negatively about others in the Kingdom of God. **We talk about people –** let me say it correctly – we gossip about people like it's a form of recreation.

We get so much enjoyment out of exposing the failures and shortcomings of others. Truth be told, it makes us take the focus off ourselves, where we are falling short and messing up. The enemy offers us stinking thinking about other people and many times we tell other people what we are thinking – that's gossiping. The best way to resist wrong thoughts is to replace the thought with the Word of God – to think or say what God says.

I remember, when I was a young Christian in my twenties, I was so excited about being saved. However, I made the mistake of being self-righteous and judgmental. I used to look at people who had "fallen short" of God's Word and not only judge them in my mind, but also share with others what I thought about them and their weaknesses.

I heard about a young lady who had gotten pregnant and was not married. Let me tell you, I had no empathy whatsoever for this woman and her situation. I could not believe that she would allow herself to be in that predicament and not be married. To me, it was the worst thing that could happen to a Christian woman. Not only did I think negatively about the woman, I also shared how I thought with others. I also looked at this woman without any compassion, even though I was a Christian, saved by grace and not living a perfect life myself. I was judgmental because I was not struggling at the time with sexual intimacy. I was puffed up, conceited and prideful because I felt like I was "doing something." I felt like I had arrived. I couldn't understand how people of faith could have struggles in this area.

Well, God has a way of helping you to understand when you say you do not understand, and are judgmental of others. That's what happened to me. God taught me how to have compassion for other people even when they fall short and how to encourage people so that they will find their way back to peace and faith in Him again.

I was taught through my own experience. God allowed me to go through some situations in my life that, had it not been for Him, I would never have made it through. As a matter of fact, the situations that I went through were so much more devastating than the ones I talked negatively about in other people.

Not only did I end up getting pregnant and not married, I went through enough hurt, pain and rejection in the process that it caused me to allow God to change my life – to move from judging others to having compassion and a desire to be more encouraging and supportive. I was so ashamed that I left home and went to my sister's home out of town. Let me not be cute with this. I ran away to my sister's house because I was embarrassed and I knew in my heart that everyone was ready to judge me just like I had judged others.

While at my sister's house, I received a call from a pastor who has since gone to be with the Lord. She ministered to me and prayed for me over the phone. By the time she was finished with me, I felt as though I no longer needed to walk in shame.

God was using my situation to get me closer to Him and to transform my heart so that I could be used by Him in the Kingdom. It took some time for me to move on with my life and not feel the pain anymore, but the closer I got to God, the less pain I felt. The closer you get to God, the less pain you will feel too.

Eventually, not only did all of the pain go away, but I was better equipped to be a witness for God and serve in His Kingdom.

Abiding in the Vine

John 15:5 says, *"I am the vine, you are the branches. He that abides in me and I in Him the same brings it forth much fruit for without me you can do nothing."* Jesus is the main Vine. He is the one who makes sure that we, the branches, are nurtured so we can produce fruit. The fruit will grow on us as the Vine feeds us.

We are in it together and Jesus is working with us. When people see our vine, they should see that we are one with Jesus because He abides in us and we abide in Him.

We read in the earlier scripture in Matthew 7:16-20 that bad seeds will produce bad trees, and bad trees will produce evil and corrupt fruit. It's a problem to bear bad fruit, but equally so to bear no fruit at all.

"I am the true vine, and my Father is the husbandman. Every branch in me that beareth not fruit he taketh away: and every branch that beareth fruit, he purgeth it, that it may bring forth more fruit" (John 15:2). God does not want us to

The world needs to see our fruit.

bear bad fruit or be barren either. With Jesus – following Him and His way – we are able to produce much fruit that may be used for Kingdom building. The world needs to see our fruit.

Benefits of Bearing Fruit

The benefits that come as a result of bearing fruit extend beyond our own personal gain. We glorify God in the process, we walk as a witness so that others can come to the Kingdom of God, and we also grow in the process of bearing fruit.

God Is Glorified. According to Matthew 5:16, we are to let our light shine before men that they may see our good works – our good fruit, our acts of love and kindness and the things we do because of Christ in our lives and the Word planted in our hearts (See Matthew 5:16).

The Bible says that, when people see these things, they will glorify our Father, which is in heaven. When we show love, which is a fruit of the Spirit, people can see it and they will glorify God. We have to give Him the credit for where we are, for our characters and for the good works that we do to ensure He gets the glory, not we.

When I was in my twenties, I used to be amazed by people who smiled and were so loving. They cared for others and demonstrated it by their actions. When they would walk into a room, they glowed and changed the atmosphere with their loving and friendly personality.

I guess I marveled at people like that because, at the time, my disposition was quite different. I so much wanted to be like that. A lot of the time, I discovered that the reason for their infectious personality was because they had a relationship with Jesus Christ and they walked in love. They were not pretending because, as you know, we often pick up when people are fake. They were genuinely and naturally loving people who lit up a room when they entered.

Although I was business-minded and ambitious, I had a desire to be as loving as they were. I wanted to move into that place and exemplify God's love, His kindness and gentleness – the fruit of the Spirit in Galatians Chapter 5. I believe that God is doing that with me when I move closer to Him. I desired what I saw in others because it was good. As a result, God is glorified.

Spiritual Growth. When we grow, we have a greater capacity to create and bring forth fruit. When you plant a seed in the ground and watch it sprout for a few days, maybe a week, you will not see any fruit. Why? The plant needs to grow and mature to the point that it can produce. If you want to be fruitful, you must grow in the Word and knowledge of Christ.

We cannot only hear the Word but we should receive it, let it grow in us and be fruitful. *"And these are they which are sown on good ground; such as hear the word, and receive it, and bring forth fruit, some thirtyfold, some sixty, and some an hundred"* (Mark 4:20). Notice, it does not say that God will bring forth fruit.

The Fruit Is Not for the Tree

We are the ones who have to hear the Word, receive it, and bring forth the fruit.

We bring forth fruit by being obedient to the Word of God. It's not just about being a good listener and hearing the Word. It is what you do with what you hear.

Accepting and following the mandate of God is the key factor in our ability to produce more. *"But be ye doers of the word and not just hearers only deceiving yourselves"* (James 1:22).

We are admonished that, when we receive Christ, we should walk in Him. Moreover, we are not built up in ourselves but we are rooted and built up in Him. *"As ye have therefore received Christ Jesus the Lord, so walk ye in him: Rooted and built up in him, and stablished in the faith, as ye have been taught, abounding therein with thanksgiving"* (Colossians 2:6-7).

> *We bring forth fruit by being obedient to the Word of God.*

How does that little sprout come up from that seed? The seed is nourished and it grows. Likewise, we are built up in Christ. We are rooted in Him. As we are sustained and nurtured by His Word, we start to bud, and the process of maturation begins. The more we walk according to the Word, the greater the capacity we have for fruit to grow on our trees. *"Abide in me, and I in you. As the branch cannot bear fruit of itself, except it abide in the vine; no more can ye, except ye abide in me"* (John 15:4). To be fruitful, we must constantly abide in Christ. How do we do that? Hearing the Word and doing the Word.

Have you ever seen an orange grow on a small sprout that came out of the ground? No. That sprout takes time to develop into a fully-grown tree. As we abide in Christ, and remain connected to Him, over time we, too, will reach a stage of full growth.

Fruitful Witness. Thirdly, and most importantly, other people will come to Christ. Why do we want to be fruitful? Why do we want to plant the Word of God in our hearts on good ground? Why should we keep our hearts in good condition? So that others may have a personal relationship with God like us. They would want to adopt our attitudes, lifestyles, behaviors and principles. They would want to serve Jesus because what they see in us is appealing and real. This is the ultimate stage of fruitfulness for a child of God. It is lifestyle evangelism – witnessing to others by living according to the Word of God.

We witness to others by living according to the Word of God.

Jesus commissioned His disciples to go and preach the gospel to the entire world. We have been given the same instructions. *"And he said unto them, Go ye into all the world, and preach the gospel to every creature"* (Mark 16:15). We have to reach others. That is our mandate as Christians.

The Fruit Is Not for the Tree

Before I understood the importance of being fruitful, I was only concerned about "me, my four and no more." I was a Christian and, as long as I went to church and received the Word, I felt that I had done what I was supposed to do. But then I reached a place where I understood that it wasn't just about me and my family. There was more to this Christian walk. I needed the Word so that I could live a life that the Lord could use to draw others unto Himself. Along the way, I have made mistakes and will go on making mistakes, but I know the truth and will strive to do what is that acceptable and perfect will of God.

Naturally, trees produce fruit to feed us. We eat the fruit and it is nourishment to our bodies. Spiritually, our lives are like trees, producing fruit to feed others. The fruit of love, kindness, gentleness, self-control and so forth will become evident in us and bring nourishment to the dryness in people's lives.

CHAPTER 2

The Condition of Your Heart

The Fruit is Not for the Tree

During a Bible study session I attended many years ago, my pastor taught on Mark 4. When she reached the verses about how the cares of the world, the deceitfulness of riches, and the desire for other things can make a believer unfruitful, and how some people "become offended" in their troubles and persecution by falling away from the Word, something leapt inside of me.

At that moment I realized that all I had gone through was not about me. There was a bigger picture. The Lord wanted to use my life as a light, to draw other people to Him – but He could not use me in the state I was in. My heart was too hard from the hurts that had me bound. I needed to be free.

I immediately began a study of Mark 4 and then later started teaching a lesson during Sunday School periodically called *"Don't Take the Bait,"* in which I taught on the Parable of the Sower and shared how God wants more from us, even when we face offenses or other challenging situations.

In the Parable of the Sower, God compares the condition of the ground the seed is sown on to the state of your heart. When the seed, which is the Word, falls on good ground or a good heart, it will produce good fruit and compel other people to want to know more about our life in Christ. Let's look at this parable from the perspective of the receivers of the Word, not the sowers.

In Mark 4:13-19, Jesus describes four types of ground (hearts) the Word falls upon. *"And he said unto them, Know ye not this parable? And how then will ye know all parables? The sower soweth the word"* (Mark 4:13-14).

Seed that Fell by the Wayside

> *And these are they by the way side, where the word is sown; but when they have heard, satan cometh immediately, and taketh away the word that was sown in their hearts* (Mark 4:15).

The first type of heart is the highway or wayside where there is no fertile soil. Can you imagine just going out to the streets, taking some seeds and throwing them there? The conditions on the wayside are not suitable for seeds to be planted. They will not take root.

Throwing seeds on the road gives the enemy an invitation to come and quickly snatch them. This is comparable to people who have not accepted Christ. They do not want to commit to allowing the seed of the Word to go deep into their hearts to take root and produce fruit. They will have none of that because they are too immersed in the marketplace.

I remember when I was growing up, there were some people who would come to church – three times a year. You could bet they would be in church when it was CME – Christmas, Mother's Day and Easter. They were not interested in having a relationship with Christ.

People with the wayside type of ground are not particularly interested in producing any fruit but, out of tradition, they go to church at those self-appointed times.

It did not matter if they had gone out the night before and got home early in the morning; they still got up, got a shower and got dressed. To them, tradition was more important than a relationship with God.

If you are not trying to develop a relationship with God to produce fruit, the enemy will take away the Word you hear, and you will not receive it for salvation.

What do people with hearts like the wayside need? One, a desire for a relationship with Jesus Christ and to accept Him as Lord of their lives. Two, after they have that relationship, they need to compel other people to come to Christ. Right now, on the wayside, they're not attracting anyone to the life of God.

Seed that Fell on Stony Ground

> *And these are they likewise which are sown on stony ground; who, when they have heard the word, immediately receive it with gladness; And have no root in themselves, and so endure but for a time: afterward, when affliction or persecution ariseth for the word's sake, immediately they are offended* (Mark 4:16-17).

The second ground is stony ground. Like the wayside, there is no root in stony ground; hence no growth and no fruit. The Bible says, "Immediately when these people hear the Word, they are excited about receiving it, but then, when persecution or trouble comes, immediately, they are offended." Offense hinders your ability to bear fruit (See Mark 4:16-17).

Have you ever seen a person who goes to church on a Sunday all excited, dancing, praising, and giving God all the glory? You see them outside the church saying, "Oh my goodness, didn't Pastor preach it! What a message!"

As soon as you ask them, "Well, what was the sermon about?" they say, "I don't know, I didn't take notes." They're excited about it but there is no root. If there's no root, then there is no fruit. In these instances, we are going to church, getting excited about the Word, the charisma, the presentation. However, the fundamental truths that are meant to create growth in our lives are not being absorbed into our system. We do not meditate on these truths and consequently cannot live by them.

It is like going to the doctor and receiving a bad report, then going to church or reading the Bible about the healing power of God – that by His stripes we are healed, yet not taking those words into your spirit. You are excited but you do not apply the Word of God to your life and situation.

Because there is no root, nothing to keep you strong and grounded, you cannot say, "Well, you know what, I know what the doctor says but I also know the report of the Lord. The Lord says that by His stripes I am healed."

What do people with stony hearts need? They need a greater desire for God, more of God, and more of His Word. They need to study to show themselves approved, so God's Word will penetrate their hearts and make them fruitful.

Seed that Fell among Thorns

> *And these are they which are sown among thorns; such as hear the word, And the cares of this world, and the deceitfulness of riches, and the lusts of other things entering in, choke the word, and it becometh unfruitful* (Mark 4:18-19).

The third type of ground is the thorny ground. This is a little different. The thorny ground has root but no fruit. The ground is partially prepared to receive the seed, but the Bible says that the thorns choke the seed and keep it from producing fruit (See Mark 4:18-19).

There are three things that choke the seed: the cares of this world, the deceitfulness of riches, and the lust for worldly things. The first thing is the cares of life. We are going to have challenges as we live this life, but our focus should be on the One who is able to bring us through; He will not leave us or forsake us (See Hebrew 13:5). God loves us, and He wants us to give Him our cares, so that He can handle them (See I Peter 5:7). When trouble comes, we can trust God and avoid living in stress and frustration.

The second thing that chokes the seed is the deceitfulness of riches. It doesn't say riches but the deceitfulness of riches, which will choke the Word and keep you from being fruitful.

> *But they that will be rich fall into temptation and a snare, and into many foolish and hurtful lusts, which drown men in destruction and perdition. For the love of money is the root of all evil: which while some coveted after, they have erred from the faith, and pierced themselves through with many sorrows* (1Timothy 6:9-10).

Notice this verse mentions, *"the love of money"* and not just money. Money is not evil in itself but, when we crave for material things, that becomes covetousness. Instead of pursuing material things, let's have a love for God, for advancing His Kingdom, and meeting the needs of God's people.

Thirdly, the lust of the flesh, the pleasures of the world, and the lust of the eyes choke the seeds in the thorny ground, so they cannot produce fruit. In Galatians 5:19-21, you will find a list of the lusts that trap us and keep us barren: from adultery, to fornication, idolatry, witchcraft, and so forth. But it says in verses 21-23, *"But the fruit of the Spirit is love, joy, peace, longsuffering, gentleness, goodness, faith, meekness, temperance: against such there is no law."* In contrast, Galatians 5:16 teaches us how to escape being choked: *"This I say then, Walk in the Spirit, and ye shall not fulfil the lust of the flesh"* (Galatians 5:16). How do you keep from walking in lust? By walking in the Spirit.

The cares the world, the deceitfulness of riches, lust, and the pride of life are all self-centered things; they are all about "me," not about doing anything for anybody else. That's why that type of life is not productive. It's like going to church on Sundays, hearing the Word, studying the Bible, and getting excited. It's true that such people obey what God says to some extent but they are not sharing God with anybody. "It's about me as long as I get mine, you get yours."

What do people with hearts like a thorny ground need? One, they need to have a desire for others to be saved and not just be concerned about their own salvation. Two, they need to witness, because again, God desires us to be fruitful.

Jesus walked by the fig tree and noticed that there were no figs on it. The fig tree had leaves; therefore, it was expected to have figs on it as well. From the outside it looked as if it was fruitful. But when Jesus went up closer, there were no figs. What did Jesus do? He cursed it because it looked fruitful from a distance but on closer look it was barren.

As God's children, we cannot just be like Christians going to church on Sunday, doing the two-step, knowing how to shout, how to dance, and how to raise our hands. What happens when there is a closer look?

When our hearts are examined, will we be in a place where we are rooted in the Word? Do we love God so much that we receive the Word in our hearts, and it takes root in good ground? Do we want other people to experience the same relationship, the same love for God that we have? Walking in offense with our hearts heavy, full of resentment, filled with anger and strife keeps our hearts in a stony and barren condition. We will not be able to receive God's Word to produce fruit.

Seed that Fell on Good Ground

And these are they which are sown on good ground; such as hear the word, and receive it, and bring forth fruit, some thirtyfold, some sixty, and some an hundred (Mark 4:20).

To recap, the seed is the Word of God and the ground is our hearts. So, the context of this parable is about the Word being received or rejected by the hearts of men for one of four reasons. What is the condition of your heart? Is it the wayside? Is it stony ground? Is it thorny ground? Or is it good ground?

The last ground is the good ground, which has both roots and fruit. These are the people who the Bible says hear the Word, receive it and then bear fruit. What is the process of bearing good fruit?

The first step is to hear the Word of God. Hearing is essential, but just hearing the Word is not enough. And so, the next step is to receive the Word. In other words, the people whose hearts are considered "good ground" accept the Bible as God's Word and believe it is the truth to stand on. They do not just know that God is a Healer but they make that declaration and personalize it, believing that God will heal them.

Knowing and believing are two different things. You know with your head but believe with your heart. Transferring head knowledge to heart belief allows you to be certain that your healing, or whatever circumstances you face, has already been dealt with by God. As a result of such faith and application of the truth, we bring forth fruit. When the Word of God is received and obeyed, we will bring forth fruit abundantly, *"... some thirtyfold, some sixty, and some an hundred-fold"* (Mark 4:20).

Why is it thirty? Why sixty? Why a hundred? The quantity of your fruitfulness is determined by your faith which translates into action. It is based on how much Word you hear, how much Word you receive and how much Word you act upon. You have to receive ALL of the seed of the Word. Don't just believe the Word concerning prosperity alone. Also, believe what it says about tithing. You cannot just choose to take one part and not the other.

Don't just believe the Word about God forgiving your sins when you confess them to Him, but also believe that we need to forgive one another. Furthermore, do not believe that we should just love God with all of our heart, soul, and mind. We must also believe Matthew 5:44, that we should love our enemies. You should have the desire to reap a hundred-fold blessing, a hundred-fold return and a hundred-fold production for receiving God's Word in your heart.

What is the condition of your heart? Don't let the enemy cause your heart to be like the wayside, stony or thorny ground. Do not allow the enemy to trap you with offenses, so you cannot focus on God and His Word. Don't let him keep you snared and bound. Make a decision not to take the bait so that your heart will be in a fertile condition, good ground that is ready to produce bountifully as the Word is planted.

Think about a tree. When you plant a seed and it gets nourishment, water and sunlight, it grows and becomes a strong tree with roots that keep it stable and fed. In time, that tree brings forth fruit. Likewise, when the Word of God falls on the good soil of our hearts, and as we are nourished spiritually, we grow and mature, producing the fruit of the Spirit: love, joy, peace, longsuffering, gentleness, goodness, faith, meekness and temperance.

The fruit on our tree will then attract other people. It compels them to come and taste its goodness. Remember, the tree bears the fruit, not for itself, but for others to enjoy. Have you ever seen a tree eat its own fruit? No. The benefit to the tree comes in the process of be able to grow fruit. God wants us to produce the fruit of the Spirit in our lives so that other people will see it and partake of it. You do not have to feel sorry for the tree, because God nourishes the tree so that it may produce the fruit. When you pursue your God-ordained purpose to be fruitful, God will lavish you with His bounty and also cause you to be a blessing in helping to bring others into the Kingdom.

CHAPTER 3

Offenses Will Come

In Matthew 18:7, we are forewarned that offenses will come, *"Jesus said, For it must needs be that offenses come."* And the Bible also tells us that in these last days people are going to become ruder and more disrespectful. So, it would be fitting to learn how to deal with offenses before they show up in our lives:

> *This know also, that in the last days perilous times shall come. For men shall be lovers of their own selves, covetous, boasters, proud, blasphemers, disobedient to parents, unthankful, unholy, Without natural affection, trucebreakers, false accusers, incontinent, fierce, despisers of those that are good, Traitors, heady, highminded, lovers of pleasures more than lovers of God; Having a form of godliness, but denying the power thereof: from such turn away* (2 Timothy 3:1-5).

The more we prepare ourselves for trials and know what to do, the better off we will be. We will, in fact, grow stronger in the midst of trials and tribulations.

When we face an offense or a challenging situation, we tend to pray and seek God more. It is to our benefit to learn from those seasons when we are on our knees. We have to remember that our problems are only temporary. The trying situation we may be experiencing with a difficult person will pass.

The challenges we face on our jobs are just for a limited period. We should be able to rejoice in that fact alone! Weeping may be for a moment but joy comes in the morning. Hallelujah!

What is an Offense?

The word "offense" in the *Merriam-Webster Dictionary* is defined as "something that causes a person to be hurt, angry, or upset." *Merriam-Webster* also defines it as something that is wrong or improper.

We cannot control the actions or words of others.

The Greek word for "offense" is "skandalon." It is the part of a trap to which the bait is attached.

It is somewhat like a mouse trap where you attach the cheese to lure the mouse. If the mouse takes the bait, it does not take long for it to discover that it was a killing machine set to destroy it.

The part of the trap holding the cheese snaps and cripples it instantly. It cannot move and will eventually die. That's the way the devil causes you to stumble. Therefore, an offense is something that intentionally tries to trap you and cause you to stumble and fall. The enemy uses offenses to trip you up and divert you from God's plan.

What does the cheese represent? It represents our ego, pride, power, selfishness and our need for revenge. It neither represents humility nor the love of God. "I've got to get the last word in. How dare he, say that to me or do that to me? I am going to pay them back." And, before you know it, you've played that in your mind a hundred times and you even contemplate what you should have said

and what you're going to say the next time the person does it. Guess what's happening? You've let the enemy get to you. That's how he traps us in our minds.

Choosing to take offense opens the door to the enemy to trap and ensnare us. He keeps us from being able to do the things of God as we should. So be warned: avoid offenses! They hinder us from enjoying the freedom to be everything God wants us to be.

Yes, the cheese looks so good to those who love cheese. It's so yummy sitting there waiting to be munched. Unfortunately, because you're concentrating so much on the cheese, you fail to see the trap. You are not aware that there's a snare waiting for you.

Unresolved hurts, living with resentment, anger and strife bring about confusion and hinder people from going further in their walk with God.

James 3:14-16 says, *"But if ye have bitter envying and strife in your hearts, glory not, and lie not against the truth. This wisdom descendeth not from above, but is earthly, sensual, and devilish. For where envying and strife is, there is confusion and every evil work."*

Inevitably, offenses will come but the problem occurs when we become aggrieved, instead of letting the action or words go. Sometimes, we rehearse what happened over and over and over in our heads. We think that the person said something degrading to us and it's not right; they're trying to show us up. We feel some "type-a way," as I call it.

Stay in Faith

We definitely need faith in order to forgive people who offend us, especially those who intentionally try to stir up anger and resentment in us. In most cases it is not easy to do so, but we can exercise our faith. God helps us know that we are to be obedient in forgiving even if we do not understand or do not want to accept the "bigger picture" because our pain or disappointment preoccupies us. Jesus helped the disciples to understand that, even though offensive behavior had consequences, they were to forgive the offenders if they repented. This was so difficult, the disciples had to ask Jesus to increase their faith so they could obey His command.

> Then said he unto the disciples, It is impossible but that offences will come: but woe unto him, through whom they come! It were better for him that a millstone were hanged about his neck, and he cast into the sea, than that he should offend one of these little ones. Take heed to yourselves: If thy brother trespass against thee, rebuke him; and if he repent, forgive him. And if he trespass against thee seven times in a day, and seven times in a day turn

again to thee, saying, I repent; thou shalt forgive him. And the apostles said unto the Lord, Increase our faith (Luke 17:1-5).

Take comfort that Jesus is ever present to help us in our time of need. Luke 22:31-32 states, *"And the Lord said, Simon, Simon, behold, satan hath desired to have you, that he may sift you as wheat: But I have prayed for thee, that thy faith fail not: and when thou art converted, strengthen thy brethren."* Just as He did for Peter, Jesus is praying for us that our faith would not falter in adversity.

We may have to go through the fire, but we must stay in faith. We are able to do so because the Lord has prayed, not against the adversities coming, but that our faith would not fail as we go through them. Take heart because He has already overcome the world. *"These things I have spoken unto you, that in me ye might have peace. In the world ye shall have tribulation: but be of good cheer; I have overcome the world"* (John 16:33).

How Do You Know You Are Offended?

How do you know you've been offended? Easy. You cannot sleep at night because you are consumed by thoughts of the situation. You play it over in your mind like a record player, contemplating what you should have said and what you're going to say the next time you are in that position. What's more, you really do not like being around the person who offended you.

Offenses start in the mind. The enemy tries to trick us in our thinking, whispering deceptive words in our ears about certain situations. He wants us to spend time worrying about the circumstances that cause us to lose the promised peace of God (See Isaiah 26:3).

Distressing thoughts about the offense affect your feelings, which are connected to your physical heart, not just your mind. God wants your heart to be in a good condition.

Oftentimes, when we are nervous or frustrated, our heartbeat becomes irregular or fast. By comparison, when we feel relaxed and confident, our heartbeats are regular.

Therefore, anger, resentment, hatred and such negative feelings are detrimental to our health. God wants to protect our hearts. That's why the Word tells us to think on God and He will keep us in perfect peace (See Isaiah 26:3).

Beyond Our Control

We cannot control the actions or words of others. But we can only control ourselves – hence, the term "self" control. There is no such thing as "others" control. Since we cannot control what other people do or say, we have to make sure that we do not lose focus or get off track when something unfavorable happens – be it an offense or a hurtful action.

You will frustrate yourself trying to keep other people from doing things and saying things that will offend you. Instead, make up your mind to be self-controlled and make sure you respond in a mature fashion to the attacks of others, so you do not lose your cool.

At some point in our lives, we all experience offenses. They could occur in your home, your family, on your job, in your neighborhood or even at church. Most of the time, we will not be able to keep offenses at bay, but we can keep them from staying in our minds and polluting our thoughts.

There is going to be a time when you have to deal with offense, but you've got to make a decision that you will not receive it. In other words, you will not hold on to what someone has said or done and become angry, upset or worried. I started teaching a class on offense many years ago at my church to encourage new members not to allow other people to divert them by their intentional words or actions to stir up anger or resentment. Rather, they should walk in love and forgiveness and stay where God has called them to be. Believe it or not, offenses cause some people to lose focus and be sidetracked. However, I encourage you not to let that happen. Even if you get angry, do not act on the anger. Instead, move forward as God leads.

When we are offended, instead of getting angry or bitter, our desire should be for God to touch their hearts and cause them to be delivered and set free. That is the mature and Christ-like thing to do.

If a person decides not to like you or not to be reconciled with you after they have offended you, then move on. You have to be okay with that. Again, you cannot control another person. You only do what is possible according to the guiding of the Holy Spirit, and then move on when a person refuses to be at peace with you. You have to keep your peace. God sees you and He will deliver you. In Exodus 3, God told Moses:

> *I have surely seen the affliction of my people which are in Egypt, and have heard their cry by reason of their taskmasters; for I know their sorrows; And I am come down to deliver them out of the hand of the Egyptians, and to bring them up out of that land unto a good land and a large, unto a land flowing with milk and honey; unto the place of the Canaanites, and the Hittites, and the Amorites, and the Perizzites, and the Hivites, and the Jebusites* (Exodus 3:7-8).

Consequences of Taking Offense

Some families are destroyed because of offenses – family members have not spoken to each other in months or even years. For some reason, they declare with pride, "Oh, I haven't spoken to her in ten years." Or "I don't play golf with him anymore." Having a relationship destroyed by offense is one thing, but it is another to glamorize or take pride in the situation. It's like a standoff – seeing who will contact whom first and apologize. It is like a Mexican showdown with family members holding grudges against one another, waiting to see who will give way first. Half of the time, people do not even remember what the other party did to offend them. After so many years, they still remember how they felt, and they still hold on to those feelings today. They are still bound by these emotions, while the other person has freely moved on with his life. Being offended is like drinking a bottle of Clorox and hoping that the other person will die.

> *The offense you encounter is only going to hurt you if you decide to take it*

People leave churches, families, and jobs because they've been offended and sometimes it is for small things. Maybe, somebody didn't speak to them or they were not invited somewhere. In marriages and relationships, a person may not put the top on the toothpaste or let the seat down – I'm talking about little things now. Some people have issues with their bosses. Perhaps, it's because she's a woman or she didn't wish them good morning.

Is It Really an Offense?

As I mentioned in the Preface, we are sometimes offended by words or actions that are not even an offense – they were never intended to cause hurt, anger or resentment. Actually, they are corrections, teachings, or words of wisdom intended to help and not hurt us. How we respond to a correction or to a true offense is important to our lives and to our witness.

Many times, when we are in the wrong lane or not walking in our "true" calling, it puts us in a position where we may have to be corrected or given wisdom in order for us to move to the place where our gifts can be used and bring glory and honor to God.

My Liberating Choice

Many years ago, I was appointed leader of the dance ministry. The anointing and power of God were tangible as we ministered in the services. Later on, however, I was going through some tough challenges in my personal life and really didn't have the bandwidth to lead the ministry as I should. Instead of stepping down voluntarily to focus on my personal life, I ploughed on.

One Sunday after church, I was told that I would no longer be in charge of the ministry. Just for a moment, I considered the action an offense and I did not feel as though it was justified. But, soon afterwards, I began to see clearly the need for me to be "sat down" for my own good. I then made a decision to rejoice in my situation. It was a very liberating choice. I chose not to have animosity towards anyone. I chose not to leave my church and I chose not to turn my back on God. During praise and worship, I would dance right from my seat, receiving

God's healing touch right there. I think I danced more from my seat than I did when I was over the ministry.

Several years later, much to my surprise, I received a call from the leadership of my church asking me to lead the dance ministry again. This time, I was ready to move forward with a new mindset: stronger, wiser and better than before. And, because of the change that occurred in me, I was able to lead the team in ministering in ways that we had never experienced before – dancing with more power and anointing. God brought restoration because I did not walk in bitterness and because I labelled what had happened to me a blessing and not an offense. It was true I needed the time away for restoration, but God had a new beginning waiting for me. He has a new beginning waiting for you, too. Let go of self-pity, let go of bitterness, and let go of unforgiveness. God will restore you and cause you to triumph!

Wandering Thoughts

Not only are some words from others considered offensive – when they are not, some actions are misinterpreted and people find themselves getting angry or resentful. We have to avoid jumping to conclusions and thinking negative before obtaining the facts. Even with just one thought you do not take captive, you can create problems that were never meant to be there.

For instance, a wife finds a florist receipt among her husband's things and immediately thinks her husband is cheating on her, since she did not receive the flowers herself. She could either banish the passing idea, or she could play it over and over in her head until the thought, just a thought, sinks into her heart and she doubts his faithfulness – even though she never had reason to before. If she lets herself doubt, she eventually assumes an attitude of criticism and anger. "I know he cheated on me," becomes easy to mutter under her breath, and she begins to carry out actions that reflect her heart.

We have to avoid jumping to conclusions and thinking negative before obtaining the facts.

No longer wanting to trust him or ask him for an explanation, she digs through his things, looking for evidence to use against him. It all came from a thought. But it consumes her.

Later, when he comes home and greets her, she treats him coldly because of the thought sown in her heart. He asks what's bothering her and though she does not answer at first, she blurts out all of a sudden, "Who did you buy the flowers for? Are you cheating on me?"

All because of an initial suspicion without any real evidence. For all she knew, he has hidden the flowers away to surprise her and show her how much he loves and appreciates her.

We can make the same mistakes when we harbor negative thoughts. We therefore have to make the decision not to allow our negative thoughts to rule us. We have to keep our own minds and spirits under control, especially when we cannot prove the negative thoughts assailing us. We must reject all slanderous thoughts and commit ourselves to learning just the facts. Once we know what is truly happening, we must choose to respond according to what the Word says in the situation, in Jesus' name, not in anger or bitterness.

There Is a Bigger Picture

God loves us so much that He sent His only begotten Son so that we would not go to hell but would have eternal life with Him – and when His Son came, He loved us so much that He forgave even while on the cross. Who are we not to walk in love and forgiveness with those around us? Who are we not to forgive our brother who has offended us? Choose to walk in the example of the Almighty God and your Lord and Savior, Jesus Christ. We have been given a Helper, the Holy Spirit, and His abundant grace.

Everyone who receives God's Son is involved in His bigger picture. His plan for me is to help me overcome offenses, so I could be in a better position to produce the fruit that would help others get to know His Son. He is the One who was the victim of all offenses but chose to walk in peace, forgiveness and self-sacrifice, not in anger, resentment or hostility. Not only did the Son come for our sakes, but God sent the Holy Spirit to comfort and guide us. Without the assistance of the Holy Spirit, trying to love and forgive people who hurt us would be a daunting task.

Again, we should walk in the Spirit so that we will not fulfill the lusts of the flesh. We have to be intentional about producing fruit in our lives so that we will be a greater witness for God. The Word will help us to stand. You have to tell yourself, *"I can do all things through Christ which strengtheneth me"* (Philippians 4:13). You also have to rise up and say, "No weapon that is formed against me shall prosper; and every tongue that rises against me in judgment, I shall condemn" (See Isaiah 54:17).

Everyone who receives God's Son is involved in His bigger picture.

The point that Christ forgave us even while He was being crucified is a truth that I will emphasize throughout this book so that readers will be encouraged to follow Christ's example of forgiveness.

CHAPTER 4

Victory Over Offenses

We cannot hold two opposing thoughts at the same time. That is double-mindedness, which makes us unstable. If you allow the enemy to cloud your mind with this silliness or that hurt because of the offense you choose to entertain, then you cannot concentrate effectively on the things of God.

The goal of the enemy is to keep your mind on the offense so that you will not have peace. But God wants you to have peace. Isaiah 26:3 says, *"Thou wilt keep him in perfect peace, whose mind is stayed on thee: because he trusteth in thee."*

If you keep your mind on God, He'll keep you in perfect peace. However, if the enemy is crowding your mind, you cannot keep the things of God on the forefront.

Now, when something is going on with you and you're uneasy and tense, you do not have peace. The enemy tries to keep you thinking about the action or words spoken and uses the offenses to confuse and manipulate you. When you do not have peace, you resort to doing things that are not of God.

Some people worry and hold on to hurt; others resort to drinking, smoking, cheating on their spouses, lying and so forth. These things can give them only temporary respite and lead them away from God.

You have to remember that the enemy is not paying rent to occupy real estate in your mind. Jesus paid it all. Jesus paid for us to have joy. He paid for us to have peace, and He paid for us to be able to think on the things of God. Resist the enemy when the negative thoughts try to linger in your mind.

Dealing with Your Enemies

When someone offends you, always remember what the Word of God says in Matthew 5:43-48:

> *Ye have heard that it hath been said, Thou shalt love thy neighbour, and hate thine enemy. But I say unto you, Love your enemies, bless them that curse you, do good to them that hate you, and pray for them which despitefully use you, and persecute you; That ye may be the children of your Father which is in heaven: for he maketh his sun to rise on the evil and on the good, and sendeth rain on the just and on the unjust. For if ye love them which love you, what reward have ye? Do not even the publicans the same? And if ye salute your brethren only, what do ye more than others? Do not even the publicans so? Be ye therefore perfect, even as your Father which is in heaven is perfect.*

The Word tells us to love our enemies (Matthew 5:44). God loved us so much that He gave His only begotten Son to die on the cross – even for His enemies. We can make a decision to love those who offend us.

When it is difficult, we can rely on the Holy Spirit to love that person through us. Therefore, we must yield to the leading of the Spirit and move according to God's plan.

We are also instructed to "*bless them that curse you.*" According to the *Merriam-Webster Dictionary*, to bless means to "praise, glorify, to speak well of or to confer prosperity or happiness upon." So, when you bless people, you release good things about them, things that cause them to prosper in their ways.

We are also instructed to "*Do good to them that hate you.*" Again, I want to stress the importance of being led by the Holy Spirit. You have to use wisdom when getting involved with people who hate you, especially if you have done nothing to provoke such emotions. For example, you may decide to take a gift to someone's house without the Holy Spirit's guidance. In a situation like this, you can encounter unforeseen challenges, which the omniscient Spirit may want you to avoid. The

> *We can make a decision to love those who offend us.*

person who hates you may not see your gesture as an act of kindness and may be offended by your benevolence. Your well-being and safety have to be considered. In such circumstances, it is essential that you allow the Holy Spirit to show you the best way to proceed when you want to do good to others.

Verse 44 also instructs us to "*Pray for those who despitefully use you and persecute you.*" When you pray for your enemies, it frees you from the bondage of unforgiveness and strife. In fact, it takes a person of faith who is rooted and grounded in the Word of God to pray for those who persecute him.

An employee may be given an unwarranted performance appraisal because of a supervisor's feelings of insecurity and intimidation. However, if that employee chooses to pray for the supervisor, it testifies of his or her faith in God, and His ability to bring deliverance and restoration.

You may not feel like loving, blessing, doing good or praying for someone who has hurt you. Nevertheless, you must allow the Holy Spirit to work through you to love others. As you extend love to those who commit the offenses, the light of Jesus within you will shine. As a result, you will touch their hearts and deter them from hurting more people.

Verse 45 is a key verse, which tells you that love and prayer are necessary, *"That ye may be the children of your Father which is in heaven: for he maketh his sun to rise on the evil and on the good, and sendeth rain on the just and on the unjust."* When we obey this command, we demonstrate that we are indeed the children of our Father in heaven, made in His image. He loved us so much that He looked beyond our faults, saw our need for forgiveness, and sent His Son as the ultimate sacrifice for sin. Therefore, when others offend us, we are to show them mercy and forgiveness.

God cares about His creation, whether saints or sinners – we should too. He makes rain fall on the just and the unjust alike. Rain is important for survival and God ensures that all mankind benefit from the rain – not just His children. In the same way, everyone benefits from the act of forgiveness – not just His children.

"Don't take the bait! Don't take the bait!" That's what you should tell yourself when all kinds of offenses happen to you. People will try to upset you for apparently no reason. They will watch your commitment to God and your close relationship with Him. The mere fact that you are taking your faith seriously and are doing good, will make some people jealous. Unfortunately, they become so enraged and consumed by envy that they look for ways to offend you and destroy your peace. However, you cannot take the bait. Do you remember when you first got saved? My goodness, how excited you were! You wanted to tell everybody that you accepted Christ and your life had changed. You were just running around, brimming with joy. You were unstoppable. But, the reality is there are people who will not like you being a committed Christian. Families, friends, and co-workers are likely to call you a "holy roller." They may be mean, laugh at you and even set a date for the end of your walk with Christ. How should you respond to those who try to steal your happiness?

The incorrect response is to curse, retaliate or react in like manner. The correct response is to love them according to the Word. It may be hard to do, but God gives us grace.

Holy Ghost Help

Sometimes it is so very difficult to forgive someone who speaks negatively about us intentionally so as to cause anger and resentment. In those times, when it is overwhelmingly difficult, we need the Holy Spirit to help us. In her book, *A Word on Love,* Ruth W. Smith teaches on how to love beyond hurt, which is allowing God to help us. "Allowing God to love through you, which is the right way to love, will transform your life."[3] The fundamental lesson is that when people are mean and say bad things about you, you can still love them with the help of the Holy Spirit.

You need the Holy Spirit's power to love them when you cannot do it yourself and your flesh is saying: "Oh no, I am not going to do this." In essence, what you are saying is, "Holy Spirit, I yield so that You may love that person through me."

...allow the Holy Spirit to lead you in knowing what to do in each situation that you encounter.

Rather than take revenge, respond with love and bless them. In other words, speak well of those who say evil about you. The good you speak is what the Bible refers to as blessing those who curse you. Even when they try to offend you, just say, "God, I am going to speak good." Better yet – pray for them.

There's nothing like praying for a supervisor who mistreats you on the job. There's nothing like praying for and blessing a spouse who is not supportive of you. Speak good words. If the individual is not saved, confess that God will provide an opportunity for someone to minister to the person so that he or she will receive Christ.

For this to happen, you need the Holy Spirit to fill you with His compassion for the lost.

Verse 44 tells us to *"do good"* to people who hate you. Well, how do you know what to do? You have to, again, be led by the Holy Spirit. If you do what *you* think you should do, it may make matters worse. Be led.

I will never forget when the Lord told me to "do good" to someone, who never spoke to me, by buying a gift to celebrate a special occasion for her child. Well, of course, I resisted at first. I did not want to walk in obedience.

The good you speak is what the Bible refers to as blessing those who curse you.

Nevertheless, the Lord spoke to my heart again, and I finally agreed. So, I purchased the gift and, when I presented it to her, she was in shock and could not believe that someone she never spoke to was blessing her family. To this day, she and her husband are amongst the people who really encourage me in ministry.

Although we are supposed to do good, in many cases, there are times when certain people should be avoided. It's biblical. *"Now, I beseech you, brethren, mark them which cause divisions and offenses contrary to the doctrine which you have learned; and avoid them"* (Romans 16:17).

Again, allow the Holy Spirit to lead you in knowing what to do in each situation that you encounter.

How Jesus Responded to an Offense

Peter denied Jesus three times even after he had experienced so much love in his three years with the Lord. Peter was renamed by Jesus Himself from Simon to Peter, which means "Rock." But even Simon Peter, the rock, denied Christ three times. Not only that, he was also called by Jesus to become a fisher of men and that's what he became.

Peter also walked on water. He was bold, yet he denied Jesus three times, wept bitterly and ran away (See Luke 22:57-62). He was offended with himself. Sometimes, when we fall short, we're harder on ourselves than others are on us.

"Peter said 'Lord, why cannot I follow thee now? I will lay down my life for thy sake'" (John 13:37). Peter was talking about his commitment, "I'm going to lay down my life for you, Lord."

"Jesus answered him, Wilt thou lay down thy life for my sake? Verily, verily, I say unto thee, The cock shall not crow, till thou hast denied me thrice" (John 13:38).

And then in John 21, knowing Peter had denied Him three times, Jesus, after His resurrection said, *"Simon, son of Jonas, lovest thou me more than these? He saith unto him, Yea, Lord; thou knowest that I love thee. He saith unto him. Feed my lambs"* (John 21:15).

In essence, Jesus was saying to Peter was, "I know you denied me. I know you wept. I know that you ran away, and I know you feel bad about this thing." But what Jesus was ultimately saying to Peter was, "I need you to get back to work for the Kingdom. I need you to get back to doing Kingdom business. Feed my sheep."

We, too, must get back to Kingdom business and not allow offenses to draw us away. It doesn't matter if we are upset about our own shortcomings; we must stay focused on God's plans and purpose for us.

In the Bible, we are given countless examples of people who chose not to be offended and won great victories for their obedience to the Word of God.

How David Responded to the Offense of His Brothers

There's David. David's father Jesse had sent him to the battlefield to bring food and he could have been offended by that menial task. Perhaps, he could have said: "You're not sending me to the battlefield so I can fight; you're sending me as an errand boy to deliver food to my brothers. What an insult!" When he got there, his brothers teased him.

Here's the point: if David had taken offense and gone home, Goliath would never have been defeated. Israel would have lost the battle against the Philistines. What a terrible day it would have been for Israel if David had chosen to walk in the offense! No one else was willing to fight Goliath with the confidence that David had. No one spoke in faith about being able to defeat that "uncircumcised dog." No one would have recalled what God had done for the Israelites in the past.

How Jesus Responded to the Offenses of the Crucifiers

Jesus, too, was offended by many. He was mocked; He was beaten; He was nailed to the cross. He had every right to be offended but instead, while He hung on the cross, He said: *"Father forgive them for they know not what they do"* (Luke 23:34). Jesus Himself decided not to take the bait of offense. He remained true to His calling, true to the prophetic word concerning His atonement, and hung on the cross for us.

Can you imagine what life would have been had Jesus taken offense and claimed His rights? "I don't deserve any of this! Get Me get down from here!" He had done nothing wrong but, because of His commitment to us, He made a decision not to be offended. It's therefore important to stay free from offenses and thus live continually in the peace of God. I want to say that, even when you are offended, you can still experience the peace of God. However, that does not mean you do not have to deal with challenging situations. It also does not mean you do not have to confront people in love. By all means do that. It just means that you will not live a life consumed by resentment and anger, which will hurt only you, no one else.

Decide that the peace of God will rule your heart from now on. Also, understand that the enemy is behind every attack. If there is an onslaught on your mind, the enemy is behind it. I'm reminded of Matthew 16 when Jesus was telling His disciples that He was going to be killed and that He would rise from the grave in three days. But Peter, in ignorance, replied: *"Be it far from thee, Lord: this shall not be unto thee"* (Matthew 16:22). At this Jesus rebuked Peter saying, *"Get thee behind me, satan"* (Matthew 16:23).

Note carefully: Jesus didn't say, "Get thee behind me, Peter." He said: *"Get thee behind me, satan: thou art an offence unto me"* (Matthew 16:23). Jesus recognized that it was the enemy causing Peter to think contrary to the plan of God. You have to realize that the enemy is behind every attack motivated by sin.

Remember, when you are tempted to take offense, it's the enemy. We wrestle not against flesh and blood but against principalities and powers. That's the enemy trying to undermine you.

Silence Is Golden

Some battles are not worth fighting. As Jesus hung on the cross, He did not answer those who persecuted him. Isaiah 53:7 says, *"He was oppressed, and he was afflicted, yet he opened not his mouth: he is brought as a lamb to the slaughter, and as a sheep before her shearers is dumb, so he openeth not his mouth."* The battle was already being won in the heavenlies, though not in the eyes of men.

In high school, I was in the Drama club, the Interact club, an honor roll student, and co-captain of the cheerleading squad. During the summer of my senior year, I made history in my hometown by winning the first NCA All-American Cheerleading Competition. For doing so, I was featured in our local newspaper. For someone who didn't have what I thought were the best looks, I felt pretty confident and was doing impressively well. In spite of all that, I was the brunt of gossip and slander during part of my high school years – I even had to look up some of the snide remarks because I didn't know what they meant.

> *Some battles are not worth fighting.*

Although none of what was being said was true, I decided to hold my peace and not say a word.

The Fruit Is Not for the Tree

In my heart, I felt sorry for the people who talked negatively about me. Furthermore, I took comfort in knowing that people defended me and didn't believe the gossip; they dismissed it as an attempt to ruin my reputation.

I must say that there were some other things about me that could have been said that *were* true – I was not perfect and definitely not without sin – but to have blatant lies spread was hurtful. By the grace of God, I got over the gossiping quick and it didn't stop me from excelling in high school academically and socially.

At the time, I didn't know what scripture to quote about not taking offense. I didn't fully understand forgiveness, and I surely did not know about help from the Holy Spirit. All I knew was that "something" inside of me helped me to move on and not worry about the gossip.

Now, I understand that betrayal and persecution is sometimes part of the plan. Judas, who betrayed Jesus, was part of the redemption plan for mankind. Judas had to betray Jesus so that He could be crucified (See Matthew 26:14-16). If there was no crucifixion, we would not have eternal life and direct access to the Father. Looking back,

I know that this experience only fueled my passion to walk in my purpose. If you are being persecuted, be encouraged. You are part of a much bigger plan.

How to Stay Free from Offense

Let me summarize the things I shared in this chapter. To stay free from taking offense, there are three things we can do: walk in the peace and presence of God, learn how to forgive, and let the offenses go.

Walk in the Peace and Presence of God. Watch what you continually think about. Don't play those offenses over and over in your head because it's only going to make you angrier. It takes too much effort to hit the rewind button in your mind and then hit play again to review what happened dung the offending situation. Put that same effort somewhere else and focus your attention on the things of God.

I repeat Isaiah 26:3, *"Thou wilt keep him in perfect peace, whose mind is stayed on thee: because he trusteth in thee."* We have to keep our minds on the things of God. Happiness comes as a result of the peace you receive when you are walking in obedience to God. Happiness is tied to being successful, and happy people function better than those who are bombarded with stress and worry due to offenses.

Do not let the years go by still stuck worrying about what someone did or said. You'll have to make a decision to let it go. You cannot have two thoughts at the same time. If you are focused on the things of God, you do not have room to let the enemy use your mind as a playground – playing mind games with you and causing thoughts to run haywire in your head.

Do not let the years go by still stuck worrying about what someone did or said.

When a person says something negative to you, naturally, it does not feel good. You can choose to respond to that person with speech that is seasoned with salt. Or you can retaliate in anger – thus missing the mark and walking in sin. Alternatively, you can spend your time pondering how you could've, would've or should've dealt with the matter. When your mind is crowded with these thoughts, you cannot think on the things of God or effectively carry on with your life. You are going off track. Is it worth it? No. The only person you are hurting is yourself. Your peace, your purpose and your provision are at stake.

Psalm 119:105 says, *"Thy word is a lamp unto my feet, and a light unto my path."* When we do not know how to move forward after an offense, we must come back to the Word and the example of Jesus Christ, which tell us to walk in love and forgiveness.

Praising God helps us to enter into God's presence. Moreover, it is our way of getting God's attention, a way of communing with God, and a way of letting God know how wonderful and how glorious He is in our lives. When we praise, we take the focus off ourselves and what we are going through for that moment. Our total focus is on God, who is able to keep us in perfect peace. God desires for us to have the experience of the Garden of Eden, the place where Adam was in God's presence to freely commune with Him.

Forgive Others. Because God forgives us our sins, we should forgive others when we are affected by their sins. *"And when ye stand praying, forgive, if ye have ought against any: that your Father also which is in heaven may forgive you your trespasses"* (Mark 11:25). Who are we not to forgive our brethren, when God has forgiven us?

Oftentimes, people allow the enemy to use them to offend others. This happens when the enemy plants thoughts in their minds to bring down others. It is unfortunate that people allow the enemy to use them to divert us from pursuing God's plans for our lives. We should recognize that the enemy is behind this, for our fight is with him. The battle in and for our minds is against satan. Ephesians 6:12 states, *"For we wrestle not against flesh and blood, but against principalities, against powers, against the rulers of the darkness of this world, against spiritual wickedness in high places."* More on forgiveness in Chapter 5.

Let the Offense Go. It's one thing to forgive, but another to forget. Some people are blunt enough to say, "I will forgive but not forget what you did." However, saying that adds no value to your life. You are only hurting yourself and remaining in bondage. Your heart becomes hardened, and the Word of God cannot effectively take root and bear fruit. Letting the offense go, means that you have both forgiven the person and forgotten the pain inflicted on you.

Who are we not to forgive our brethren, when God has forgiven us?

You do not expect that person to "pay" for the wrongdoing against you. As far as you are concerned, the offense has been thrown into the sea of forgetfulness as God does when He forgives us. He not only forgives but *"He will turn again, he will have compassion upon us; he will subdue our iniquities; and thou wilt cast all their sins into the depths of the sea"* (Micah 7:19). More information about dealing with the pain of an offense will be shared in Chapter 7.

Ask the Lord to heal your heart so that you will not be like that person who drinks Clorox, hoping that somebody else will die. The poison you take will harm you, no one else.

After I was divorced, I had a difficult time adjusting to being single again and honestly, I did not want to end my role as a stay-at-home mom. I enjoyed being very active in my children's lives and being available to volunteer at their schools. I didn't have time to heal and to be totally restored because I had to take care of my children and go to work. I worked in a couple of positions that were not right for me at the time and I was let go. Being fired from a job was not something I was used to as I had always received high ratings on jobs in the past.

Both situations could have been devastating, but I had to put my trust in God and believe that He had something better in store for me. More importantly, I made up my mind not to leave either situation blaming other people and bad mouthing the job or any of the employees. Sometimes, things change and you are no longer a good fit, personalities clash or maybe your season in a particular place may have just come to an end. Whatever the reason for the termination or resignation, as it may be with some, it is best to leave in peace.

In both situations, God said, "I want you to love the people and, if you do, I will elevate you." At first, this was one of the hardest things I've ever had to do in my life, but I remembered who was speaking to and guiding me. If I couldn't trust God, who could I trust? Well, I did it. I made a decision not to put my mouth negatively on the job or anyone there. I went on with my life to complete my Master's Degree in Business, and my publishing business escalated. Above all, I heard God tell me to walk in forgiveness as He had a work for me. Remarkably, as it turns out, most of the references and letters of recommendation that I now use for contract or regular employment, come from those two jobs – where I was let go. Imagine that! When I think of the goodness of Jesus, I rejoice. I have letters from a vice president at both places of employment endorsing me. Who ever heard of someone being terminated from a job and then receiving recommendation letters? But God! He gave me favor.

Look Beyond the Offense. Understandably, looking past an offense is much easier said than done. Feelings of hurt, disappointment and anger can be overwhelming and, at times, it is difficult to see beyond our emotions. Jesus was the perfect example in that He did not focus on the cross. He looked beyond the cross even while He was on it towards the joy that the cross would bring.

> *Looking unto Jesus the author and finisher of our faith; who for*
> *the joy that was set before him endured the cross, despising the*

> *shame, and is set down at the right hand of the throne of God* (Hebrews 12:2).

Jesus looked forward to the joy of fulfilling His purpose, instead of focusing on the transitory agony He was experiencing. He understood that very day, He would sit at the right hand of God the Father. He knew that mankind would have a pathway back to God through salvation, and He would return to receive His bride – the church.

One of the two men hanging on the cross beside Jesus admitted that Jesus had done no wrong as they had, and he asked Jesus to remember him in His Kingdom. Jesus responded in the affirmative: the man would be with Him in paradise. Jesus looked past His pain and focused on the joy – the paradise ahead for Himself and for the man who reached out to Him.

> *And one of the malefactors which were hanged railed on him, saying, If thou be Christ, save thyself and us. But the other answering rebuked him, saying, Dost not thou fear God, seeing thou art in the same condemnation? And we indeed justly; for we receive the due reward of our deeds: but this man hath done nothing amiss. And he said unto Jesus, Lord, remember me when thou comest into thy kingdom. And Jesus said unto him, Verily I say unto thee, Today shalt thou be with me in paradise* (Luke 23:39-43).

Don't look at the offense and your present pain; look to your future! See the joy that will come as a result of your obedience and commitment to walk in humility, prayer and love.

Stay in Faith. Faith is believing that God will bring into existence those things that are not yet seen: *"Now faith is the substance of things hoped for, the evidence of things not seen"* (Hebrews 11:1). We can hope for positive relationships with others in the midst of being offended. That's what faith causes us to do.

The Bible states that we should walk in faith "above all." *"Above all, taking the shield of faith, wherewith ye shall be able to quench all the fiery darts of the wicked"* (Ephesians 6:16). Faith helps us to quench or to put out the fiery darts of people who are walking contrary to the Word of God. Faith causes us to be strong despite the enemy attacks.

Jesus told Peter that satan desired to sift him as wheat (See Luke 22:31). In other words, the enemy wants to shake up our lives so much so everything we stand on is destroyed and what remains is of no use to use. But note that Jesus prayed, not for satan not to sift us, but that we might have unshakeable faith: *"But I have prayed for thee, that thy faith fail not: and when thou art converted, strengthen thy brethren"* (Luke 22:32).

We have to walk in faith, seeing those things that are not as though they were. We have to look to a brighter future.

It's a Choice

If you choose to say yes to an offense, you are choosing to entertain it. When you take that cheese on the mousetrap, you fall for the enemy's tricks. The part of that trap, which represents the offense, will snap and pin you down. The mechanism is such that, once you grab that cheese, you cannot move. Offenses will cripple you and make it difficult for you to progress in the things of God.

> *Offenses will cripple you and make it difficult for you to progress in the things of God.*

I pray that you will not allow offenses to ensnare and trap you. Instead, you will walk in the love of God and yield yourself to the Holy Spirit, so you can love people even when it's hard to do so. God bless you! We should desire to be fruitful so that others will be compelled to Christ. Since we desire to live an abundant life, physically, emotionally and spiritually, we cannot allow the pain of the past to keep us from bringing forth fruit now. Even for those who do not struggle with the pain of the past, situations in the present can quickly stifle their fruit.

The first line of attack by the enemy is our thought life, so watching what we think is incredibly important. When a negative thought enters our heads, we have to expel it right away before it can take root. When you let a thought – even an impression – linger in your mind, it begins to color the way you look at everything. But when you drive that thought away, set it loose, then you do not give it a chance to alter your reality.

When we choose to dwell on negative thoughts, they worm their way into our hearts. Once inside the heart, they affect the fruit we produce. We start to feel more and more negative until our attitude sours. We develop anger and other strong emotions because the idea harbored in our head and heart changes our perception of the world.

"Out of the abundance of the heart, the mouth speaks" (Luke 6:45). The words you speak will accompany the negative thoughts you have let fester. Even with just one thought you do not set free, you can create problems that never had to exist. We have to make the decision to not allow our thoughts to rule us, but to walk in love. We must purpose to keep our own minds and spirits under control, especially when we cannot prove the negative thoughts assailing us. We must reject all slanderous thoughts and commit ourselves to learning just the facts. Once we know that the evil is truly happening, we must choose to respond according to what the Word says regarding the situation, not in anger or bitterness.

You are Not a Victim

For a long time, I acted like a victim because of what I had endured as a child. I looked like a victim even though I may have been dressed up nicely. It was easy for me to be the target of ridicule. It was easy for me to be the target of laughter and to be picked on for any reason, especially the wrong reasons.

I began to realize that I and people like me – timid, insecure and lacking in confidence – were an easy target because the offender figured, "Well, this one's not going to fight me back. This person already does not have a good self-image. She looks like she doesn't value herself, so why should I?" So, we were open to attack until we made up our mind we were no longer going to be victims. In Christ I am a victor! Hallelujah!

You're a victim because you do not know who you are. You do not know whose child you are. But once you do, you will come into the realization that who you are is not dependent upon what you look like and what you do and what you act like. Who you are depends on who you have accepted as your Lord and Savior and what He has done for you. It's about Him and so, stand up and tell yourself you're more than a conqueror through Christ Jesus.

When we come to the realization that we are children of the Most High God, that we're joint heirs with Jesus Christ, then we allow our God to lift up our heads and make us walk tall.

Never again will we see ourselves as losers. Never again will we cast away our confidence, in the name of Jesus. I decree and declare that we are no longer the victim. We are the victor.

Back Off from the Way of Offense

Sometimes, through our own negligence, we put ourselves in the path of offense, that is, we open ourselves to being hurt or disappointed by someone else. How many times have we heard "a voice" saying to us, "He is not the one," "Don't get involved with that person," "Walk away"? And we do not listen. It is the voice of the Holy Spirit trying to keep us from going a certain way where the offense is sure to happen.

We can avoid potential trouble if we are obedient. But the thing I love about God is that, even when we do not heed to His warnings, He still extends mercy and allows every situation that we go through to work for our good (See Romans 8:28). God is able to do exceedingly abundantly above all that we ask or think. (See Ephesians 3:20). So, even when we think that we are undeserving of His mercy, grace and forgiveness, He shows us how loving He really is and why He sent His very own Son to die for us. Who wouldn't serve a God like that?

CHAPTER 5

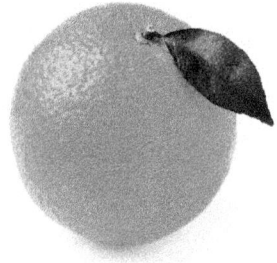

Forgiveness Is Not an Option

Walking in forgiveness is something we all need to embrace and practice as a lifestyle if we want to be submitted to the Word of God. Our freedom in Christ depends on our ability to forgive others for the wrongs they've done us.

Forgiveness is the act of pardoning an offender or someone you love who has hurt you. Forgiveness involves not bringing up the offense against the offender again. I'll even go further and say that, as Christians, granting forgiveness is not optional.

We must do it as instructed in Matthew 6:14-15, *"For if ye forgive men their trespasses, your heavenly Father will also forgive you: But if ye forgive not men their trespasses, neither will your Father forgive your trespasses."*

It is important to understand that, although forgiveness is not an option, each person should seek God about what to do or how to go on once he has forgiven. Do you leave, do you stay, do you continue to do business, do you seek monetary compensation if appropriate, or do you seek justice? These are questions that are posed by Christians daily. Know that there is no one-size-fits-all solution when it comes to how you move forward. The Holy Spirit who guides should be sought for direction as you study God's Word.

Experiencing hurt at some point in our lives – is a fact of life. But, even so, you have to keep on living. Just know that, when you forgive someone who hurt you, you are not excusing their behavior. You are setting yourself and the other person free.

Shouldest not thou also have had compassion on thy fellowservant, even as I had pity on thee? And his lord was wroth, and delivered him to the tormentors, till he should pay all that was due unto him. So likewise shall my heavenly Father do also unto you, if ye from your hearts forgive not every one his brother their trespasses (Matthew 18:34).

Who Hurt You?

Who are the people who hurt you? If you write a list, it would probably be very long. It might have included your spouse, a family member, a friend, a co-worker. It could even have been a church member. Unlike what you may think, you can get hurt in the church as you work alongside other Christians. None of us is perfect and, from time to time, everyone, no matter how righteous we consider them, will fall short of God's standards.

Society itself can be a major source of disappointment, anger and resentment. The fact that our society is more open, tolerant, and accepting of ungodly standards and values, may offend and hurt many.

Words are powerful instruments for good or evil.

"How did we get to this point?" "How could these things go on?" "How could people not see the things that are wrong?" We battle with these questions daily, and many people who try to take a stand are criticized and belittled.

How Do People Hurt You?

There are countless ways that we can be hurt by another person – intentionally and unintentionally. These are a few of the ways.

Negative Words. The Bible says that words are spirit and life and can be used to help or hinder, encourage or discourage, build up or tear down. Words are powerful instruments for good or evil (See John 6:63). Unfortunately, too many times, we use words to hurt and offend. We say mean things, speak lies and criticize for no good reason. If you are a parent, you know how it feels when someone says something bad to your child. That hurts and you may be quick to retaliate. One of the most detrimental ways is gossip, which is often associated with the deceit of people smiling in your face and saying bad things about you behind your back. Some people even have the audacity to tell bare-faced lies and total untruths. Verbal abuse is equally distressing and damaging to all of us. Words have the power to release life or death over you (See Proverbs 18:21).

Physical Abuse. Sometimes, offense happens when a person is physically abused, perhaps, in a domestic violence situation. Or at school, somebody may pull your hair, push you down or bully you. That hurts. It is difficult to look at a person the same way, especially after being physically abused, because the pain extends beyond our emotions.

Being Left Out. People can leave you out intentionally or inadvertently. But the net result is the impression you did not count. They may invite everyone in the room to an event, except you. You end up being the lone ranger. Perhaps, everybody got an envelope but you didn't get one. You're out in the cold.

Belittling. You may have been treated like you were stupid or ignorant. Sometimes, you may be working with others and they act like you really cannot think. That's a pet peeve of mine. We must allow people room to make mistakes. A supervisor used to say to me, "If you are not making any mistake, you are just truly not doing anything."

Rejection. Rejection is a major source of hurt. It is true that hard times reveal your true friends. Very often, we find ourselves in situations where the people we expect to be there for us, leave us. They prove they were fair weather friends after all, who were there in the good times when you had a lot of money or when you were rolling, but when the bad times hit, they turn their backs on you.

How Do You Feel When You Are Offended?

Angry. Yes, you are angry. Sometimes, you feel your anger boiling into rage. But Ephesians 4:31-32 says, *"Let all bitterness, and wrath, and anger, and* *clamour, and evil speaking, be put away from you, with all malice. And be ye kind one to another, tenderhearted, forgiving one another, even as God for Christ's sake hath forgiven you."* The Bible also says, *"Be ye angry, and sin not: let not the sun go down upon your wrath: Neither give place to the devil"* (Ephesians 4:26-27).

We are going to get angry sometimes, but it is important to understand that we must not let our anger take control of us. When we let our anger sit and fester in us, we have already opened the door to the entry of all kinds of evil spirits, including tormenting spirits.

Resentful. Resentment is a feeling of indignation. You know you have feelings of resentment when just seeing a particular person tears you up on the inside. Even though you may think you have good reason to store up these feelings, you are only hurting yourself. In fact, harboring anger and resentment could eventually kill you.

Sad. Another emotion that presents itself is sadness. My tears are a sure sign that I am hurting. Those close to me know that when I start to cry, I am feeling intense pain in my soul, and they know it's time to back off.

However, extended sadness is not natural and can lead to depression. It's normal to grieve over a tragedy, for grieving is part of the healing process – but only for a season. *"To everything there is a season, and a time to every purpose under the heaven ... A time to weep, and a time to laugh; a time to mourn, and a time to dance"* (Ecclesiastes 3:1,4). But to hold on to perpetual grief is detrimental to your body and soul.

Disappointed. Disappointment is inevitable in life. At some point, those we love and expect much of will fall short because we are all imperfect and fallible. People will fail us, even the ones who made genuine promises and had good intentions. When this happens, you feel disappointed and sometimes ashamed as if you were played for a fool. You may not be angry but you do not want to be associated with the person who caused you so much hurt.

Vengeful. It has been said that hurting people hurt other people. Those who hurt are sometimes consumed with the desire to take revenge to get back at the person hoping it would soothe the pain. If I'm hurting, more than likely, I will want to hurt somebody else. Who better to hurt than the person who hurt you? Or if I cannot, how about someone associated with him in some way?

What does the Bible say about revenge? *"Dearly beloved, avenge not yourselves but rather give place unto wrath: for it is written, Vengeance is mine; I will repay, said the Lord"* (Roman 12:19).

Who will repay? God says, *"Vengeance is mine."* What happens when we get to a place where we want revenge? By taking matters into our own hands, we show we are not trusting God to act on our behalf. We are literally taking ourselves out of His hands, out of His protective shield.

Forgiveness Does Not Mean …

Forgiveness does not mean that you are condoning a wrong done or that you are accepting of another person's sin. It also does not mean that you have to be reconciled to the offender and continue in the same relationship you had before. Furthermore, it also does not mean that you are denying that the person is responsible for hurting you. However, you are choosing not to hold it over that person's head, to make that person pay you emotionally, and sometimes tangibly, for what they've done because you have forgiven and let go.

Understand this: although people who offend you do not owe you anything for being granted forgiveness – not even an apology – it does not mean that, in some cases, they will not have to pay for or deal with the consequences of their actions in some other way.

For example, if two people are having an argument and one of them throws the other's cell phone on to the floor, although the person forgives the other, it does not mean that they will resume normal communication as if nothing happened. It does not mean either that the person who broke the cell phone will not have to replace it.

It is important to add that, even though you forgive the offender and they owe you nothing with regards to your restoring your peace, it does not mean that they will not have to answer to God or to the authorities for their actions.

In a movie I watched recently, a family forgave a young girl for killing their child in a car accident. Although the young girl was forgiven, she still had to face the courts in terms of her driving record and incarceration.

However, the family received the peace they needed when they decided to not only forgive, but to let go of any expectation of justice being served for their pain. This will not happen in every situation because every situation is different. Let God be the ultimate judge in everything. Seek Him.

What You Should Do

Forgiving someone for offending you can be one of the most difficult things you will ever have to do, especially if the words or actions caused you great pain. However, these tips will make the process easier for you to be obedient to the Word of God.

Forgive Quickly. The first thing we need to do is to quickly forgive so that God can forgive us (See Mark 11:25). The Greek word for forgiveness has the sense of letting go of. Decide to let go of the hurt and pain. Give it over to Jesus as the Bible instructs us, *"Casting all your care upon him; for he careth for you"* (1 Peter 5:7).

Think about Jesus as He hung on the cross – the ultimate Forgiver. He said, *"Father forgive them for they know not what they do"* (Luke 23:34). Even hanging on the cross with nails in His hands and feet, He still had enough love in Him to forgive those who had offended and persecuted Him.

Give it over to Jesus as the Bible instructs us.

Release the Offender from Guilt. A lot of times when we are offended by someone, we still hold that guilt against the other person. But, when we truly forgive somebody, we release that other person from guilt completely.

When God forgives us, does He still hold on to our sins? No, He doesn't. When we go to Him, and confess our thoughts and sins, the Bible says that He is faithful and just to forgive us and then He purifies us from all our unrighteousness (See 1 John 1:8-9). He doesn't hold it over our heads. As far as the east is from the west, He has removed our transgressions from us (See Psalm 103:12).

It's like being in a courtroom: the person found not guilty sees the judge hit that gavel and hears him say, "Not guilty. You are free to go." It's done. That person cannot be tried again because he has been exonerated from the crime.

As Christians, can we go a step further and say to our offenders, "Even though you are guilty, I am not going to hold this thing against you anymore. I'm not going to remind you of it either" It does not mean that the person did not commit the act. But the penalty is gone. You are not condoning what they did but you are freeing them and yourself from bondage. Nevertheless, you should note that forgiveness does not mean there are no consequences for the offender.

David was forgiven by God after he repented of his sin with Bathsheba and the murder of her husband (See Psalm 51). However, the consequences of that sin on his family were devastating.

Give the Benefit of the Doubt. Sometimes, we should not take the things people say personally as they may have been having a bad day and said something without thinking. Or they may be going through a challenge – sickness, divorce, grieving the loss the loss of a loved one. Sometimes, it's just about showing mercy. *"Blessed are the merciful: for they shall obtain mercy"* (Matthew 5:7). The Bible also says, *"Good sense makes a man restrain his anger, and it is his glory to overlook a transgression or an offense"* (Proverbs 19:11, AMPC).

In the Daily Hope online devotion, Pastor Rick stated, "Not everyone who bugs you or hurts you realizes what they're doing. Oftentimes they're responding to their own hidden pain, and they don't even know that they're hurting all these people around them."[2]

Walk in Love. As I mentioned in a previous chapter, we have to love and forgive others. *"But I say unto you, Love your enemies, bless them that curse you, do good to them that hate you, and pray for them which despitefully use you, and persecute you"* (Matthew 5:44). *"For we wrestle not against flesh and blood, but against principalities, against powers, against the rulers of the darkness of this world, against spiritual wickedness in high places"* (Ephesians 6:12). Your real enemy is not the person who hurt you. Your enemy is the devil who instigated the whole conflict. He knows your vulnerabilities and will use words or situations to stab you in just the right places. He will try to create strife with the other person and, when you take the bait, he will cause you to brood over the wrong done and keep you in perpetual bondage. The moment you forgive, you are released from that trap.

What You Should Not Do

Constantly Brood over the Offense. When somebody hurt you or said something you did not like, did you want to hit back with a cutting remark? Later, you may find yourself rehearsing in your mind what you will tell them the next time they say anything like that. Have you ever been in such a position – playing it over and over in your mind?

Guess what's happening? When we constantly role-play these things in our minds, we are hurting ourselves continually. That's the tactic of the enemy to confuse our minds and steal our peace by thinking about the negatives, instead of occupying our minds with the things of God.

So, what should we fill our minds with?

Your real enemy is not the person who hurt you.

> *Finally, brethren, whatsoever things are true, whatsoever things are honest, whatsoever things are just, whatsoever things are pure, whatsoever things are lovely, whatsoever things are of good report; if there be any virtue, and if there be any praise, think on these things* (Philippians 4:8).

If we want lasting peace that does not elude us in times of turmoil and distress, we need to constantly fill our mind with things that are good and lovely and praiseworthy. If we choose to meditate on the downside of life, we will be in a constant state of agitation. This reminds me of Saul in the Bible when he was disobedient to the Lord and God was displeased with him.

Saul was tormented. He tried to find peace by having David play the harp for him. But the peace he found was transient: when the music faded, so did his peace (See 1 Samuel 16).

Use the Offense Against the Offender. Prime examples of what happens when we use the offense against the offender are found in marital situations. If a husband, at one time, used money for gambling instead of taking care of household expenses, then the family suffers.

When the husband seeks help and receives deliverance from gambling, then the wife should not bring up his former habit every time they have a disagreement. If she has forgiven her husband of the offense, harping on it will only make matters worse.

How Joseph Responded to Offenses

Joseph was Jacob's favorite son. As a token of that love, Jacob gave Joseph a coat of many colors. But that coat became an offense to Joseph's brothers. What became even more offensive to them was that Joseph had two prophetic dreams elevating himself, which he shared with his brothers.

So out of jealousy they threw him into a pit and later sold him sold into slavery to some traders on their way to Egypt. In Egypt he worked as a slave in the home of Potiphar. There, Potiphar's wife accused him of attempted rape for which he was thrown into prison, in spite of his innocence (See Genesis 37).

Joseph was eventually freed from prison and brought to the palace of Pharaoh because he could interpret dreams. Here he gained favor and rose to the position of second in command after Pharaoh, governing the whole of Egypt. Due to his prophetic insight, grain was stored after every harvest as provision against the predicted famine.

The famine did indeed come upon the land, but Egypt had ample supplies enough to supply the whole region. Some of the Israelites went to Egypt for food. Guess who were among those looking for food? The same people who threw him in the pit – his brothers (See Genesis 39-41). The tables were turned. Now, Joseph's brothers needed refuge and food. Joseph gave them what they needed, and he was reconciled with his family (See Genesis 42-47).

What We Can Learn from Joseph

Joseph's offences were the training ground for his maturity and success. Joseph went from being sold into slavery to becoming a powerful leader in Egypt. He had grown from being a spoilt brat in his father's house to becoming a prominent national figure because he had learned to overcome offense in the face of setback after setback. In the process, he had developed a spirit of excellence.

When his brothers came to Egypt during the famine looking for food, he had every opportunity to have his revenge on them. In his position of power, Joseph could have said: "Hey, remember when you all threw me in the pit? Have you any idea how much I have suffered because of you?" That is not what Joseph did. He chose to walk in forgiveness. He loved them and allowed them to settle comfortably in Egypt, followed by many from his homeland, and they all prospered.

I believe that, if Joseph had been resentful and decided to live in bitterness, all of God's plans for his life might have been aborted or he might have been diverted from his purpose of being a blessing to his family and to the land of his adoption. Notice that it wasn't immediately that the brothers came to Joseph to ask for mercy. It was only after their father had died that they humbled themselves and asked him for forgiveness. But, even at that late stage, Joseph still chose not to take offense. His response was, *"But as for you, ye thought evil against me; but God meant it unto good, to bring to pass, as it is this day, to save much people alive"* (Genesis 50:20).

That was the bigger picture. If Joseph had never been sold into slavery and if he had not been unjustly thrown into prison, he would never have developed the character to rise to such a place of prominence in Egypt, second only to Pharaoh. He could not have shared his wisdom to Pharaoh to plan and strategize for the expected famine. He would never have had the grace to forgive his brothers and to cause his family to settle in Egypt during the famine. All those lives would never have been saved if Joseph had not been magnanimous. Joseph faced all these adversities for the greater good.

The Bible tells me that everything works for our good – not some things – everything. *"All things work together for our good"* (Romans 8:28). Sometimes, we do not know why we're hurting. We do not know why God allows it. Many times, there is a greater good because God is trying to accomplish something greater than we can imagine. There is a larger plan and purpose. And forgiveness is a major part of that plan, opening a way to the flow of God's river of abundance.

As the light of the world, I challenge you that, if anyone has hurt you, walk in forgiveness. I encourage you to put that person in your prayers. I encourage you, if the Holy Spirit leads you, to do good to that person, to bless that person with your mouth – do it! Don't go around bad-mouthing them because that means you are still holding them in the bondage of guilt. Instead, bless them with your words and, like Joseph, you will experience God's amazing favor come upon you.

CHAPTER 6

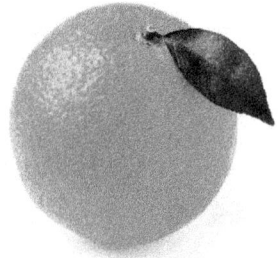

Your Life Is a Witness

The Fruit Is Not for the Tree

To me, there's nothing more spiritually rewarding than accepting Jesus Christ. When many of us received salvation, we were so excited, so pumped up. We wanted to let everybody know how happy we were. We wanted to share our faith with other people. We wanted to witness and let them know about the Christ we accepted and served.

As you make this Christian journey, it's important not to lose your excitement, because along the way, offense is capable of souring you up. You will experience situations that are not so sweet. But it's important to always go back to the joy you felt when you first got saved, when you were so enthusiastic about sharing our faith with others. We wanted to continue doing so because that is what it's ultimately all about –witnessing for Jesus, advancing His Kingdom, opening the eyes of the blind to see Jesus.

Bearing fruit is the activity that actually compels other people to come to Christ. When we show love and forgiveness, Christ is able to draw people unto Himself (See John 12:32). Will you willingly produce fruit, even in adversity, that will compel others to know more about your life in Christ? He is ready to draw those who see the fruit in your life.

Has anybody ever said or done anything to you that required an equal response? Perhaps, you were laid off from a job or faced a severe challenge. But your Christ-like response caused those looking on to marvel about how you managed in your crisis with such peace and grace. It was only possible because of your relationship with Christ. Your attitude and actions opened the door for people to wonder who caused you to have such peace and joy in the midst of trials. That's how we witness with our lives.

It's not just about turning the pages of the Bible and telling people what the books of Matthew and Romans say. It's also about our very lives and the light and fruit that comes from us. People see that fruit and want to partake of it. They see it; it looks good, and they believe that it will be good for them, too.

When we choose to agree to do things Christ's way, not to be offended and walk in love and forgiveness, our hearts are better prepared to receive the Word and to receive it on good ground. When the Word falls on good ground, it brings forth fruit – some thirty, some sixty and some a hundred-fold. But if the Word falls by the wayside, on stony or thorny ground, it will not produce the fruit that attracts others to Jesus. They will not want to know Him because they see nothing particularly winsome in us.

We All Need Forgiveness and Salvation

Because of sin, we all need salvation. It goes back to the Garden of Eden when Adam and Eve messed up and God had to implement His redemption plan to bring mankind back to Him.

Remember, the Garden of Eden represents the very presence of God. That's where He had placed Adam and Eve close to Him and with direct access to Him.

Have you ever had direct access to somebody who was in high authority such the president of a company, whom you could visit anytime without a pass?

To connect directly with somebody without having to go through another person is a privilege. Adam and Eve had that privilege – straight access to God. But when they disobeyed God by eating of the tree of the knowledge of good and evil, they had to leave the Garden of Eden. They were removed from God's presence and lost their communion with God.

Because of Adam's sin, all mankind inherited a sinful nature. In other words, we were all born in sin. The Bible says, *"Wherefore as by one man, sin has entered into the world and death by sin; and so death pass upon all men"* (Romans 5:12). It also says, *"For all have sinned"* (Romans 3:23).

God Sent His Son

God already had a plan for our salvation. He loved us so much that He sent His only begotten Son not only to save us but to reconcile us to Him. *"For God so loved the world that he gave his only begotten son that who so ever believe in him shall not perish but have ever lasting life"* (John 3:16). When we believe in His Son, not only do we receive everlasting life, we can also be reconciled with the Father and communicate directly with Him through praise, worship, prayer and meditating on His Word.

1 Corinthians 15:22 says, *"For as in Adam all die, even so in Christ shall all be made alive."* When we accept Christ, we are able to live again. We are new creations in Christ and walk in newness of life (See 2 Corinthians 5:17).

Jesus witnessed on this earth, drawing many to Him through His teachings and miracles. His disciples continued His work of witnessing throughout the world and bringing many to Him. Guess what? It did not stop with Christ; it did not stop with the disciples. We are also charged with going out and telling people about Jesus Christ so they will also experience salvation, everlasting life and have direct access to the Father.

We are new creations in Christ and walk in newness of life.

The Bible mentions an episode of how Jesus invited Himself to dinner at the home of Zacchaeus, a tax collector, a man despised by his own people because of corruption. Jesus embraced this tax collector and proclaimed, *"For the son of man came to seek and to save that which was lost"* (Luke 19:10).

Jesus was seeking, not only Zacchaeus, but the sinful world, where He had come to seek and to save the lost.

The work of salvation has not stopped with Jesus or His disciples. We, too, have been called to the Great Commission of sharing the gospel of Jesus Christ and making disciples so that the lost would be saved (See Matthew 28:18-20).

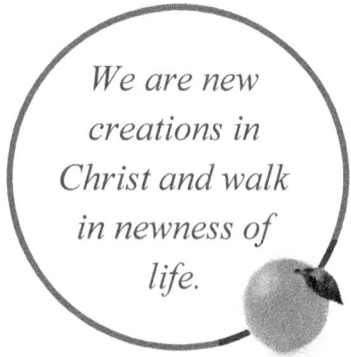

As Jesus taught His disciples, so are we to preach the gospel and make disciples. Now the work of witnessing is in our hands. *"Then Jesus said unto them, Peace be unto you. As my father hath sent me, even so I sent you"* (John 20:21).

Remember, God so loved us that He sent His Son. And so, Jesus is saying, "As my Father has sent me, so also am I sending you. I need you to go and do what I've done: to bring in the lost, to help them from drowning in their sin."

Christ Sent the Holy Spirit

"And when he had said this, he breathed on them, and saith unto them, Receive ye the Holy Ghost" (John 20:22). We cannot go into the world and witness with the same love and compassion of Jesus without the power of the Spirit of God. Witnessing means sharing the gospel of Jesus Christ in the hope that people will accept Him as Lord and Savior. In other words, we are leading people to Christ. I want you to understand why it's so important that our hearts remain good ground because of our primary purpose while on the earth. Before He ascended into heaven, Jesus told His disciples that, as His Father had sent Him, so, too, was He sending them. And then, He breathed the Holy Ghost upon them. (See John 20:22)

Not only does Christ breathe on us the Holy Spirit the day we are born again, we are baptized into His power to go out into all the world and be faithful witnesses of Jesus. *"But ye shall receive power, after that the Holy Ghost is come upon you: and ye shall be witnesses unto me both in Jerusalem, and in all Judaea, and in Samaria, and unto the uttermost part of the earth"* (Acts 1:8).

The Two Greats

Our love for Jesus Christ for what He did should cause us to act, to do something. What is that something? To carry out what I call the "Two Greats."

The first "Great" is the Great Commandments: to love God and to love others as ourselves. The second "Great" is the Great Commission where we witness and compel others to Christ after the sending forth: *"Go ye therefore…"*

Great Commandments. *"Jesus said unto him, Thou shalt love the Lord thy God with all thy heart, and with all thy soul, and with all thy mind. This is the first and great commandment. And the second is like unto it, Thou shalt love thy neighbour as thyself. On these two commandments hang all the law and the prophets"* (Matthew 22:37-40).

First, you are to love God with all of your heart and with all of your soul and with all of your mind. Then He says, "Love your neighbor as yourself." These are the Great Commandments from Jesus.

Great Commission. The Bible says, *"Go ye therefore, and teach all nations, baptizing them in the name of the Father, and of the Son, and of the Holy Ghost: Teaching them to observe all things whatsoever I have commanded you:*

and, lo, I am with you always, even unto the end of the world" (Matthew 28:19-20).

Earlier in His ministry Jesus had called His disciples, *"Follow me, and I will make you fishers of men"* (Matthew 4:19). Jesus showed the disciples how to fish for people by loving and forgiving others. His ultimate love and forgiveness were exemplified as He hung on the cross, beaten and bruised. Even in that state, He said, *"Father forgive them; for they know not what they do"* (Luke 23:34).

Who are we not to follow the example of Christ?

He loved even in the midst of persecution and offense. Who are we not to follow the example of Christ? God so loved us, He sent His Son. Because we so love Christ, we ought to love God and others and lead them to Jesus Christ.

Many people have come to know Jesus Christ because of what He as well as His disciples did when they were persecuted. The disciples also faced trials and afflictions because they were faithful witnesses. Like them, as witnesses, we will also be troubled and offended at times. What must we do? We must do as Jesus did: love, forgive and continue to be witnesses.

Think about the twelve disciples. They all were busy in their professions but Jesus told them, *"Come and follow me. I will make you fishers of men"* (Luke

4:19). Immediately, they dropped their nets to follow Christ because of the example He had set.

Is there anyone willing to follow you because of your godly example, the love or the forgiveness and mercy you are showing? Have you led anybody? Have you compelled anybody to Christ because of the fruit you bear? Has anybody seen your fruit? Has anybody wanted to partake of the fruit you manifest in your character by coming to know the Jesus you serve, having a relationship with Him and accepting Him as Lord?

And now, Jesus is sending us. He has taught us how to move forward as witnesses. He has taught us how to be witnesses with love, forgiveness, kindness and care for people. He has taught us how to do it and, because of our love for Jesus Christ and what He did for us, we are now willingly go forward to carry out the two Greats: the Great Commandments to love God and to love other people and the Great Commission to go into all the world and tell people about Jesus Christ.

2 Corinthians 5:14-15 says, *"For the love of Christ constraineth us; because we thus judge, that if one died for all, then were all dead. And that he died for all, that they which live should not henceforth live unto themselves, but unto him which died for them, and rose again."*

It is not about us. It is about Jesus Christ. We must love and forgive as Jesus does. We have to walk in forgiveness and, when people offend us, we have to see the bigger picture, that our lives are to be witnesses of Christ in us, and bear fruit. It's also about the condition of our hearts. Don't allow offenses to turn your heart into thorny and stony ground. Instead, let the Word fall on good ground, take root and flourish so that other people can see the Christ in you, and glorify God.

CHAPTER 7

Back to a Place of Peace

When we have experienced hurt through offenses that cause disappointment, anger or resentment, it is essential for us to get back to a place of peace. In this world, we are often in turmoil within and without, and we need the peace of God to live on a higher plane.

Have you ever been obedient to God concerning forgiveness, yet still struggled and lacked peace? We all have. It's like cutting your finger. You may have applied the ointment, the bleeding has stopped, and the shock of the injury is over. But you still have to deal with the nagging pain in your finger as a result of the wound.

You want to get to the place where your soul is free from pain and, in time, you know it will come. But what do you do in the meantime?

Is it possible to forgive someone who has hurt you and still not have total peace because of the pain? I ask this question because of my own experience. When I went through the process of being betrayed in a relationship, I felt like I was suffocating from tightness in my chest. I wanted to click my heels so that I could have peace again and stop experiencing the deep pain that I was going through.

Be Sober and Vigilant

We cannot be effective witnesses if we are unstable and overwhelmed by the issues of life. When your peace is disturbed, it affects your ability to be sober-minded and vigilant as God desires. You find it difficult to think properly, to be alert, sharp, to make correct decisions and exercise good judgment. Lack of peace can also affect your mental ability and cause paranoia, making you think that things, people and situations exist to hurt and disappoint you.

The bottom line is the enemy wants to devour you. *"Be sober, be vigilant because your adversary, the devil as a roaring lion, walketh about, seeking whom he may devour"* (1 Peter 5: 5-8). Know that he will use anybody or anything: co-workers, family members, neighbors, friends can all be weapons in his attempt to sabotage your walk with God and your calling. You would be naive to think he would not attack you. If you're on God's track, the devil will do everything in his power to stop your good works.

When you are not sober and alert, it leads to the wrong responses to situations. Don't react in the wrong way. There are many people who resort to drugs and alcohol or enter into wrong kinds of relationships when their peace is disturbed. Because they are not thinking soberly and their judgment is impaired, they find themselves getting involved with someone they didn't want to be with, in the first place. When the issues are resolved and peace is restored, they wonder, "What in the world was I thinking?"

> *When you are not sober and alert, it leads to the wrong responses to situations.*

We have "Did I do that?" moments, doing things that are outside of the will of God. They may be good things, but not God things. All because we're wrapped up and drawn away by trying to numb the hurt, trying to make ourselves feel better and trying to fix it ourselves, instead of allowing God to fix it for us.

Sometimes, God allows situations in our lives to free us from such things. Yet, we work diligently to hold on to what God is trying to liberate us from and end up hurting ourselves and drifting further into a place of no peace.

Moving Towards Peace

The Lord told me that, in order to come out of my own state of distress, I had to do what His Word said regarding forgiveness. But before I could even get to the point of forgiving, I had to humble myself and walk in love. It was so hard at first, but I finally said, "Yes," to God. Admittedly, I did not arrive at that place of peace right away, but here's what I did. These points have been emphasized throughout this book.

Humility. I had to humble myself. When you walk in humility, it means you are allowing the Holy Spirit to lead you. You stop rationalizing the situation and thinking of your own plan of restoration. When you humble yourself and stop thinking that "your way" is the way, then you become more sensitive to the Holy Spirit and what He is trying to say to you through the Word, in prayer and through others. Humility will help you to love again.

Love. Love means that, despite what this person did, I am going to love him unconditionally with the love of Christ. I am not going to hate him anymore, but I'm going to allow God to do a work in me and to show me what to do. When we truly love a person, we say and do what God says in His Word. The Word enables us to search our own hearts and discover the deeper things He is calling us to: *"Deep calleth unto deep at the noise of thy waterspouts: all thy waves and thy billows are gone over me. Yet the Lord will command his lovingkindness in the day time, and in the night his song shall be with me, and my prayer unto the God of my life"* (Psalm 42:7-8). Let that be our desire, too.

Forgiveness. As mentioned so many times throughout this book, God commands us to forgive. After you have humbled yourself and decided to love as God loves you, then you are ready to forgive your offender and no longer harbor bitterness in your heart When we remember what Christ did for us even while we were sinners, it should be so much easier to forgive. Anger and resentment, holding people hostage and making them feel indebted to us should not be our right anymore. The offender has to answer to God, not to us. We have to release him and walk in forgiveness. As soon as we do, we position ourselves to be in a better place to regain our peace.

Forgiveness means the person owes you nothing. It means that the person does not have to repay you anything for your personal satisfaction. Whether he apologizes privately or publicly or offers some recompense, or none at all, none of that is required for your peace to be restored. You make a decision to forgive regardless of his actions.

Understanding Peace

The *Merriam-Webster Dictionary* says that peace is a state of tranquility or quiet; it is freedom from disquieting or oppressive thoughts. I emphasize "freedom from disquieting or oppressive thoughts." Because the enemy oppresses us in our minds and then our actions follow. He tries to attack our thoughts and emotions, and to rob us of that peace.

Again, you have to focus on God, for He will keep you in perfect peace (See Isaiah 26:3). The Hebrew word for peace is "shalom." Shalom means to be complete and to be sound. *"For God has not given us the Spirit of fear but of power, of love and of a sound mind"* (2 Timothy 1:7).

Today, I confess you have a sound mind. I don't care what it is you're going through; your mind is sound and you are operating in the perfect will of God. Continue to believe that and trust God. He has given you a sound mind so that you can walk in peace, not in fear, but in the faith that He will see you through the challenge.

The Greek word for peace is "eirene," which refers to rest and tranquility. Peace is the outcome of walking in obedience to the will of God. Isaiah 32:17 says, *"And the work of righteousness shall be peace and the effect of righteousness, quietness and assurance forever."*

Romans 5:1 says: *"Therefore being justified by faith, we have peace with God through our Lord Jesus Christ."* How do we have peace with God? Through the finished work of our Lord and Savior Jesus Christ. "

For he is our peace, who hath made both one, and hath broken down the middle wall of partition between us" (Ephesians 2:14). Christ is our peace; He has broken down the partition, the middle wall between us and God. He shed His blood for us so we may have direct access to the Father to receive His peace in any situation.

> *Peace is the outcome of walking in obedience to the will of God.*

He told His disciples that He had to leave this earth. But His love for us is so great, He promised the Holy Spirit, our Comforter. The Lord resides within us; we are not alone. He will never leave us or forsake us. He leaves us with these comforting words:

> *Do not be anxious about anything, but in every situation, by prayer and petition, with thanksgiving, present your requests to God. And the peace of God, which transcends all understanding, will guard your hearts and your minds in Christ Jesus* (Philippians 4:6-7).

The enemy desires to sidetrack us. He desires to trap us through situations, through people and also through our thoughts, but we now know how to get back to a place of peace.

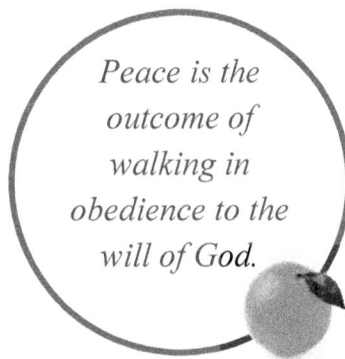

Two Things to Remember

As you go through your transition, I'm certain these two things will bring you comfort and assurance, and lessen the pain. The first thing to remember is that all things work together for good.

> *And we know that in all things God works together for good to them that love God, to them who are the called according to his purpose* (Romans 8:28).

All things work together for my good – not just some things, not just the good things – everything. As my daughter always says, "Good or bad, it's going to be good." Therefore, it doesn't matter what we go through; we know that it's going to be for our good. God will make sure of it according to His Word.

The second thing to remember is that God will make a way of escape for you.

> *There hath no temptation taken you but such as is common to man: but God is faithful, who will not suffer you to be tempted above that ye are able; but will with the temptation also make a way to escape, that ye may be able to bear it* (1 Corinthian 10:13).

Hallelujah! God will provide a way out if the pain is unbearable so that you can overcome. Glory to God! You can stand through whatever you are facing today or in the future.

If we can just remember those two things, it will help us to see the light at the end of any tunnel. It doesn't matter what your problem or your circumstances may be; God has promised that it will work for your good and He will not let you be tempted beyond what you can bear.

If you can keep these truths in the forefront of your thoughts, life's challenges and afflictions will not destroy you. You will be more able to stand in the place of peace, trusting God and knowing that everything will work out alright.

Stop Playing the Victim

God delivered the children of Israel out of Egypt. However, they started to complain every time they experienced challenges and began to yearn to be back in the same place of slavery and affliction (See Exodus 12-15). Some of them had the unmitigated gall to say, "We should have stayed in Egypt. Because of all that we are doing right now and where we are going, why did we have to leave Egypt?"

Tell yourself that you will not continue to look back to the things that kept you bound...

How could they have forgotten that Egypt was the place of their captivity, where they were the slaves of the Egyptians and severely oppressed? How could they look back to that place of bondage? Only because they were influenced by the lies of the enemy. He does it again and again. If he can persuade us to look back to that place of enslavement and oppression and see it as a better place, he knows we will never progress in the things of God.

The devil is a liar! Say that to yourself today. Tell yourself that you will not continue to look back to the things that kept you bound and incapacitated. God wants us to progress; He wants us to go forward but we can't do that by dwelling on the past.

In the physical, no matter how hard you try, it is impossible to walk forward and backward at the same time. Likewise, in the spiritual – we have to remember to look forward. We have to look to the hills from where we get our help (See Psalm 121:1).

We have to trust in God for better days ahead.

Even when we have been exemplary Christians in terms of walking in love, humility and forgiveness, there is one practical strategy to get over the hurt and that is to stop playing the victim and beating yourself up.

Stop the would-have, could-have, should-have syndrome – if I could have, if I would have, if I should have or I should have done … then things would have been different. You have to stop all of that and stop feeling guilty.

Some of us carry guilt around and think that we should have done better or handled the situation differently. What's done is done. You can't change the past, but you can look to your future.

Back to a Place of Peace

I went through a situation recently, and reached a point where I felt that what I was going through was my fault. But, it was like the Holy Spirit stopped me in my tracks and said: "Don't own that! Don't own that!"

I began to thank God because I had been receiving the lie from the enemy that I was the only one to blame.

When the enemy attacks, he targets our minds and brings thoughts to us that make us feel even worse than the situation merits. You don't have to own what the enemy says. Tell him, "I will not own that! That thought will not be my thought!" Get rid of it.

In my own life, I still had to deal with the prolonged aftermath of the betrayal. I still felt enormous pain and disturbing thoughts. I did know that the pain in my heart mainly stemmed from allowing myself to constantly review the situation.

I continued to try to figure out why I was betrayed. I thought about "what could have been" and battled with tremendous disappointment.

In many wrong ways, I was attempting to fix what could not have been mended at the time. To be honest, I was not trusting God to guide my life. Rather, I was using my lack of peace to justify my regrets and my actions.

We just have to learn to let go and let God take over.

Dealing with the Pain

After we go through various challenges in our lives, whether we are offended, disappointed, hurt, or did not get what we wanted, we have to get back to the place where we're not brooding over those experiences. In other words, we need to stop rehearsing the bad events in our minds over and over again. Because when we do that, we hinder ourselves from moving forward.

You cannot effectively move forward by looking back. Recognize the enemy's strategy of making you dwell on your past failures, heartbreaks, bad choices and anything that will steal your peace, and make a firm decision to cut that out.

...think on the things of God even in the midst of dealing with your challenge.

I challenge you to be single-minded: think on the things of God even in the midst of dealing with your challenge. Yes, we have to grieve. Yes, we have to deal with it. Yes, there's pain. Yes, we are angry because of our circumstances at times. But we have to get over it. We have to move beyond our circumstances and push towards a better position.

Although offenses are intended to bring hurt, resentment and pain, there is another side that will benefit the victim of the offense. When we experience the pain of offense, oftentimes it will cause us to get closer to God – seeking Him in prayer more and declaring His Word over our lives more. We are at a point where our only hope of restoring peace is being in the presence of the Almighty God. It is only when we set our minds on God that He can keep us in a place of peace to be used by Him as effective witnesses on this earth.

Respond Instead of React

You must purpose to respond only to God's plan. Notice that I did not say "react." When we respond, we make rational decisions, which are well thought out and informed. Who is our informant? The Holy Spirit. He will let us know what we should do in situations if we yield to Him and desire His wisdom. Instead of reacting on impulse, without thinking or seeking God, let Him guide you. Sometimes, our proper response may be immediate and other times, it may take hours or even days according to what God says. The important thing to remember is to respond, rather than react.

In doing so, we allow God to have His say in the matters of our heart. Matthew 5:4 says, *"And I say unto you love your enemies, bless them that curse you, do good to them that hate you and pray for them which despitefully used you and persecute you."* We have been instructed to do four different things in this one verse: love, bless, do good, and pray.

In your particular situation, what is God calling you to do? When you bless somebody, do you speak good words about the person? When you do good, do you do it as the Holy Spirit guides you? Of course, you can go to God and pray on another person's behalf, but the key is what did God ask you to do? Sometimes, when you are in a place where you do more than God requires of you, you get in His way.

We often try to fix something that He does not want us to fix. He wants to fix it Himself. When we are in a painful situation, He may be asking us to just pray, not to try to do anything, not to try to work it out – just pray and then move on. He wants you to move out of the way to protect you.

You cannot see that He's protecting you because you cannot see the big picture. But He can. So, when the rubber hits the road and the debris starts falling, you are not in harm's way. God loves us so much that He'll move us when certain things happen. Again, He wants to protect us, and so what we have to do is tell Him "Thank You."

Trust God in advance if you know why He's moving you out of the way. Trust God in advance if you know or do not know why you're going through your problems. I used to say that you will understand better by and by. But can you trust Him before the by and by comes? Go ahead and thank the Lord in what you're going through so that you can go back to your place of peace of mind, body and spirit.

It's all about trusting God and allowing God to be our refuge and our deliverer. Regardless of what another person does or says, we can trust God to take us to that secret place, where we feel loved, appreciated and beautiful in Him. I give God praise today for what He has done for me.

Practical Steps to Restoring Peace

Some offenses are quite easy for us to get over, but there are those that hit us like a "Mack truck" and it takes more time for us to experience total peace again because the pain is just so deep. These are some practical steps that I took when I experienced a very painful broken relationship. Leaning on the Lord and following these steps helped me to have peace again and truly be in a place where I desired for the other person to be blessed and to get closer to God in their daily walk.

Smile. Go ahead. Try it. Something happens when you smile. You immediately feel better. In those moments where the enemy tries to bring the offensive situations back to your mind, begin to smile. It is though you are letting the enemy know that you are on to him and he will not win.

Replace Negative Thoughts with Positive Thoughts. You will find this suggestion throughout this book because bombarding our minds with negatives is one of the enemy's chief strategies. Negative thoughts lead to negative feelings. Negative feelings can lead to negative actions. And, we want to avoid acting on our anger as it affects the ground of our heart and causes us to be unfruitful.

Focus on Jesus and the Word. He is living on the inside of you. You've got to give Him praise for who He is. Remember what He has done for you. Not only did He shed His blood, He also sent His Confidante, the Holy Spirit, who gives us the peace we need. The Holy Spirit is the Comforter. Pray, praise, study the Word, and keep the Word in your ears. While facing challenges which caused me tremendous hurt and pain, I kept the Word of God in my ears. I listened to sermons and prayers on audio and video. I would also sing with my daughter, whose songs are inspired by the Word of God.

Sing. Whenever I am going through something that is a little heavy, I sing a song entitled, "Tis So Sweet" as I walk through the house. When I get to, "Oh, for grace to trust Him more," I am so caught up in the presence of God that my load seems a little lighter. I also sing with my daughter, who writes songs that are inspired by the Word of God. It was my pastor who told me to sing. So glad she did!

Give Thanks. Give thanks to God in whatever it is you're going through. *"In everything give thanks for this is the will of God in Christ Jesus concerning you"* (1 Thessalonians 5:18). Giving God thanks shows that you trust Him in every circumstance, and He will give you the peace to escape each trap.

No matter what you're going through, just begin to say, "Father, I thank You for what I'm going through as I know that all things work together for my good. Although I may not be able to see what good will come out of this situation, I choose to walk by faith and thank You for working it out for me. Thank You for Your very present help in this situation."

Thank God for bringing you out. Thank Him for how He is making you better, even though you may not be able see all of His magnificent handiwork at the moment.

Conclusion

I want to close with the words of Jesus about abiding: *"Abide in me, and I in you. As the branch cannot bear fruit of itself, except it abide in the vine; no more can ye, except ye abide in me"* (John 15:4).

We should keep these words locked in our hearts. Unless we abide in Him and He in us through His Word, we can do nothing. We cannot produce fruit, we cannot deal with offenses, we cannot witness.

We should thank God for the good work He has already started in our lives and for His abundant grace in helping us deal with situations and people we thought we were incapable of handling. Others would have lost their minds, so praise God for the abundance of His spiritual blessings!

Writing this book not only helped me handle offenses more appropriately, but it also helped to be more sensitive to the feelings of others. I began to think about the people I had hurt, disappointed and offended over the years, many times unintentionally, and came to the realization that I needed to do a better job also at not causing offense - hence, the subject of my next project. Sometimes, we don't understand the impact of our words or actions on others until we experience the very same hurt ourselves.

Pray for people who have intentionally disappointed you, hurt you or offended you. Pray that they would allow God to have His way in their lives.

We will know we have reached a new place of maturity and peace when we desire no ill for the people who hurt or offended us. The day we stop rehearsing the wrongs people have done both in our minds and verbally is the day we have come out of it. Release them and let them go, so you can live happily and peacefully, bearing fruit that the world needs to see.

Again, this journey is so much bigger than us.

About the Author

C. D. Dudley's life encompasses all of these roles: author, songwriter, producer, philanthropist, adjunct professor, management consultant, publishing executive, leadership strategist and licensed minister. She is the President and CEO of More Excellent Way Enterprises (MEWE), a multi-management operations firm that provides book publishing, assessment planning, management consulting, and professional development services.

Dudley holds a Bachelor of Business Administration degree in Management from Georgia State University, and a Master of Business Administration degree from South University, graduating with the highest honors. In spite of spending part of her childhood in one of the most notorious districts in Atlanta City for gang activity, she relentlessly pursued her ambition with the support of family and teachers, and managed to graduate from high school and college. With over 25 years' experience in post-secondary education instruction and administration, she firmly believes in the value of life-long education.

Dudley has a passion for music and children. She is the founder of The Judah Awards that honors ministers of music. She has produced four CD-in-a-Book learning programs for children under the Sing with Me Bible Series: Bible ABCs, Bible 123s, Bible Colors and Bible Colors. In addition, she has written and produced over 70 songs and other praise songs, including "Walk it Out by Faith" and "God Will Do Amazing Things" for her children's programs. She is the Executive Producer of the emerging, interactive, children's show, Bible Boogie LIVE as well as the Founder of the Future Success Kids program that inspires elementary-school children to think early about their career options through a fun-filled and educational workbook and sing-along CD. She is also the lyricist for the Alma Mater for a technical college.

As a member of a ministry in Metro Atlanta, Dudley has served in various capacities, including Lighthouse Ministry Director, Children's Choir Director, Dance Ministry Director and Multi-site Ministry Director. In addition to her career and ministry positions, Dudley is fully committed to philanthropic causes. She has supported breast cancer survivors and breast cancer awareness for over fifteen years through annual donations. She also aspires to provide financial support and resources to parents and children, and for many years has assisted low income families on governmental assistance to obtain gainful employment by providing assessment, life-skills and various training opportunities.

Dudley has four children who fully support her in ministry. She loves traveling with her family and encouraging, not only her own children but other children through her various ministries, to know God and hold on to His unchanging word, no matter what the challenges. Ever ready to share her testimony with others, she declares that she is a victor, not a victim, no longer bound by the events of her past but walking in newness of life with her Shepherd, the Lord and Savior Jesus Christ.

C. D. Dudley
Book Signings • Speaking Engagements • Product Information
thefruitisnotforthetree@gmail.com
www.thefruitisnotforthetree.com
www.mewellc.com

Other Titles by C. D. Dudley

Visit
www.mewellc.com
to order copies
TODAY!

Endnotes

Johnson, Lorie. "The Deadly Consequences of Unforgiveness." CBN.com (beta). June 22, 2015. Accessed October 1, 2017. http://www1.cbn.com/cbnnews/healthscience/2015/june/the-deadly-consequences-of-unforgiveness.

Smith, Ruth W. A Word on Love: Discover the Power of Allowing God to Love through You. Lithonia, GA: MEWE, 2009.

Warren, Rick. Cut People Some Slack. April 24, 2017. Accessed October 1, 2017. http://pastorrick.com/devotional/english%2fcut-people-some-slack?roi=echo7-30321473916-50905852-c4c47325b9da689d0835d5735df144fd&.